PROVERBS
The Blessings of Wisdom

A Bible Study Guide Journal
for Women & Men

By:
CHRISTOPHER S. COOPERSMITH
Part of the *Guiding Scripture* series

GET A FREE EBOOK: THE THREE LETTERS OF JOHN & JUDE, DAILY PROVERBS CHECKLIST, 5 QUESTIONS TO FULLY UNDERSTAND A BIBLE VERSE, A LEADER'S DAILY CHECKLIST, AND EXCLUSIVE CHRISTOPHER COOPERSMITH MATERIAL!

Get these resources for free by signing up for the mailing list.

1. A Guide to *The Three Letters of John & Jude* – free eBook
2. Daily Proverbs Checklist
3. 5 Questions to Fully Understand a Bible Verse
4. Leader's Daily Checklist

Plus, Exclusive Christopher Coopersmith Material!

TABLE OF CONTENTS

About the Book 5

Sample Reading Plan 6

Community Guide 7

Tips on How to Build Community 8

Yahweh, God, Lord 10

Who Wrote Proverbs? 11

Who Was King Solomon? 12

How Did King Solomon Become so Wise? 13

Kings Solomon's Sin 14

The Book of Proverbs 15

Proverbs 1: The Fear of the Lord 16

Proverbs 2: Flee from Immorality 22

Proverbs 3: Trust in the Lord with All Your Heart 27

Proverbs 4: A Father's Instruction 33

Proverbs 5: Cherish Faithfulness 39

Proverbs 6: The Folly of Indiscretion 44

Proverbs 7: Warning against Adultery 50

Proverbs 8: Wisdom Calls from on High 55

Proverbs 9: Folly Shouts Out 62

Proverbs 10: Two Paths – Righteous vs. Wicked 67

Proverbs 11: The Fruit of Righteous Living 73

Proverbs 12: Diligence and Discipline 79

Proverbs 13: Walking with the Wise 85

Proverbs 14: The Reward of Honest Work 91

Proverbs 15: Words That Speak Life 97

Proverbs 16: Ruling One's Spirit 103

Proverbs 17: Flee from Strife 109
Proverbs 18: Death and Life in the Tongue 115
Proverbs 19: God's Counsel Prevails 120
Proverbs 20: Mind Your Company 126
Proverbs 21: Why Pray for Your Leaders? 132
Proverbs 22: A Good Name 138
Proverbs 23: Beware of Covetousness 144
Proverbs 24: Do Not Envy the Wicked 150
Proverbs 25: Set Clear Boundaries 156
Proverbs 26: The Fool, the Sluggard, and the Gossip 162
Proverbs 27: Guard Your Assets 168
Proverbs 28: The Rulership of the Righteous 174
Proverbs 29: Have Self-Control 180
Proverbs 30: God's Word is Complete 186
Proverbs 31: The God-Fearing Woman 193
Summary: 199
Want More? 200
Author 202
Other Titles by Christopher Coopersmith 203
ACKNOWLEDGMENTS 205
Copyright 2022 206
Bibliography 207

About the Book

This book is a very simple way to read God's word through the next 31 days (or more). Proverbs is a book centered on "wisdom," and it is presented in short, simple, understandable terms. By following the will of God, we acknowledge that God simply knows best.

The teachings of Proverbs are intended to lead us to pursue righteousness in all aspects of our lives. We are to strive for godly character and to live outside of our selfish desires. To gain God's wisdom, we are to place ourselves humbly under the authority of God. We, as Christians, ought to read the book of Proverbs to obtain daily, practical wisdom on how to glorify God in our everyday life.

This Guide is to assist in learning essential, everyday wisdom from the inspired word of God. Each chapter contains a personal commentary, sharing insights from the Holy Spirit during my study of the scripture.

Themes of the Book of Proverbs

    The Fear of the Lord Brings Wisdom
    The Value of Knowledge and Heeding of Instruction
    The Importance of Humility in Life's Situations
    The Consequences of Pride
    Contrast between Wisdom and Folly
    The Folly of Excess
    The Wages of Idleness

Sample Reading Plan

Reading the Bible is a personal and ongoing journey. There is no "right way" to do it. It is important to pray and reflect on scripture as you go through your everyday life. Here are some suggestions to help you get started:

1. Begin with Day 1 and aim to read a chapter each day.

2. Before reading the chapter, take time to reflect on the commentary at the beginning, and pray for guidance.

3. As you read the chapter, choose the one verse that resonates with you the most.

4. Write down the verse on the following page, and journal about how you feel God is speaking to you through the verse.

5. Repeat this process each day, allowing God's Word to speak to your heart and guide your thoughts and actions.

Remember that reading the Bible is a personal experience. Take your time, reflect, and allow the Holy Spirit to guide you on your journey.

Community Guide

God's Word is the good news to be shared with all people. As believers, we can equip ourselves with the knowledge to continually bless one another just as "iron sharpens iron." Our relationships with Christ and the church are built through prayer, support, encouragement, and ministry. This Guide is an excellent resource to connect with others and apply the teachings of God's Word to our own lives.

Together as a family, we can deepen our understanding of God's Word. Community allows us to grow together in our faith as a Christ-filled body spreading the love and grace of God to everyone we meet as lights in a darkened world. Let us embrace this opportunity to connect with one another as we serve the Lord together.

Tips on How to Build Community

Assign a Group Leader: Prior to each meeting, assign one person to lead. This can be decided by the church leadership, the organizer, or a group vote. The leader should determine how the study will be organized and outline the objectives for the day. They can also appoint a co-leader(s).

Limit Group Size: This guide is a powerful tool for building relationships, so everyone should have the opportunity to connect with others. If you have a large group of ten or more, consider breaking into smaller groups of three for more personalized prayer and discussion.

Social Media Usage: A social website is a great way to create private group pages and invite friends to participate in a Guide group.

Meet Anywhere: We should never limit ourselves to the confines of a church building. Your home and public places can quickly turn into houses of worship. In today's digital world, a "meeting" can also be a video conference.

Times to Meet: The format of the book is to meet daily and discuss each chapter. However, this routine can be flexible, such as meeting every two days, weekly, monthly, etc.

Encourage Congregation Participation: In this method, the chapter is read before the regular service. One or two people will discuss how God spoke to them. After the service, there should be an allotted time for members to discuss this in more detail. They can be assigned a group or a partner, and they can meet in a general area. This method allows everyone to have the opportunity to participate.

If you do not have a community, please send an email to gs@christophercoopersmith.com to join fellow believers in our private Facebook group.

YAHWEH, GOD, LORD

The scripture portion of this book is taken from the World English Bible Translation (WEB), which is in the Public Domain. Although God has many names and titles throughout the Bible, this translation refers to God as Yahweh. Each of God's names reveals something unique about His character. Moses may have revealed Yahweh as God's name to the Israelites. Judaism has always maintained the worship of Yahweh as the one true God, and it has not replaced Him with any other deity.

WHO WROTE PROVERBS?

As you read through the book of Proverbs, you will see King Solomon is the confirmed author. However, there are reasons to consider that Solomon did not write chapters 30 and 31, due to the Proverbs stating two different authors. There is also a style change. It is possible Solomon used a pseudonym, although there would be no real reason for this. Solomon implies that he collected some of the recordings from various sources. In Proverbs 22:17, King Solomon speaks about "the words of the wise," indicating it may have come from someone other than himself. Solomon was a man of experience, and God may have inspired him to write based on the lessons he learned personally.

Chapter 30 names the writer as "Agur, son of Jakeh," who could have been an associate or student of Solomon. The relationship was similar to that of a favorite student and their teacher. There is little evidence outside the Bible about who Agur was or where he came from. Agur means "compiler" or "knowledgeable" in Hebrew, which could be interpreted as the contents being compiled by Solomon using a symbolic name.

In Chapter 31, King Lemuel is named the next author. Lemuel means "devoted to God," "for God," or "belonging to God." There are no known records of his existence in Israel or the surrounding regions. However, he credits his mother with teaching him the contents.

Who Was King Solomon?

King Solomon, reputed to be the wisest man in history, was the son of David. He was blessed with great prosperity in the early years of his reign over Judah. Solomon was appointed heir by King David, even though he was not the eldest son.

King Solomon built the first temple in Jerusalem and served as the last leader of a united Israel. Solomon would fall in love with a woman, possibly his first wife, and the expression of pure marital love as ordained by God is detailed in the Song of Solomon. The Song of Solomon outlines their relationship, including their courtship and marriage.

How Did King Solomon Become so Wise?

Most of us dream of God asking us what we want directly, but God already knows our needs and desires before we ask. At the same time, many of us are filled with our own desires. In a dream, God told Solomon, "Ask for whatever you want me to give you" (1 Kings 3:5).

Young as he was, Solomon asked God not for money or power, but for a discerning heart: "So give your servant a discerning heart to govern your people and to distinguish between right and wrong. For who is able to govern this great people of yours?" (1 Kings 3:9).

God was pleased when Solomon asked for understanding and granted his request, adding "riches and honor" as well. Under Solomon's reign, Israel would economically flourish as Solomon built commercial relationships with the neighboring kingdoms. He used his prosperity to construct a magnificent temple for the whole nation to glorify God.

Kings Solomon's Sin

Unfortunately, Solomon would grow to love women more than he loved the Lord, who bestowed many gifts upon him. He married over 700 women and had over 300 concubines. Some of the women were foreign and worshiped false gods. These sinful relationships would cause him to build temples to false idols.

These affairs significantly affected his relationship with the Lord. Eventually, Solomon's heart was turned away from the Lord and went after other gods. Toward the very end of life though, he turned back to serve the only one true God and rejected the false idols. Out of grace, God would redeem Solomon, who would go back to believing in having only one wife.

"Live joyfully with the wife whom you love all the days of your life of vanity, which he has given you under the sun, all your days of vanity, for that is your portion in life, and in your labor in which you labor under the sun" (Ecclesiastes 9:9).

The words in Proverbs are inspired by God to take to heart the wisdom shared by King Solomon himself. Solomon was a sinner, just like you and me. Although he failed to serve God with a full heart, he found restoration with God's forgiveness.

The Book of Proverbs

Proverbs 1: The Fear of the Lord

The first chapter of Proverbs opens by verifying King Solomon as the principal author and stating the purpose of Proverbs: "that the wise man may hear and increase in learning." Solomon then makes the bold assertion that the fear of Yahweh (God) is the beginning of knowledge. However, this fear is not to be confused with being afraid of the Lord as a punisher. Rather, it means being in awe of Him. This fear is expanded in Proverbs 9:10 as "the knowledge of the Holy One is understanding."

Wisdom is the answer in life's choices. Even in the direst of circumstances, we can depend on Proverbs to guide us right where we are and shield us from calamity.

It therefore makes sense that Solomon would open his book of Proverbs speaking about wisdom. But what's crucial here is his discussion of "the fear of the Lord." Here we learn to draw a fine line between healthy and unhealthy fear.

These two kinds of fear are either unproductive or productive. Unproductive fear arises when you are afraid of something beyond your control, like the state of the nation's economy, politics, or layoffs, and that fear puts a serious strain on you. That's unhealthy fear.

On the other hand, healthy fear is productive because it propels positive action. Let's say your concern about the state of the nation's economy causes you to create a more manageable budget and save a little extra money. The fear then doesn't put a serious strain on your life, and you are able to live free from the stress it is causing. That's healthy fear causing you to be productive!

Having a solid understanding of healthy vs. unhealthy fear helps us to rest assured that true wisdom comes from the fear of the Lord. It is with this understanding of fear that we can acknowledge His ultimate power and authority over our lives. This is the basis of all wisdom and forms the necessary foundation we need to interpret the rest of the book of Proverbs effectively.

Proverbs 1: Scripture

The Beginning of Knowledge

1 The proverbs of Solomon, the son of David, king of Israel:

2 to know wisdom and instruction; to discern the words of understanding;

3 to receive instruction in wise dealing, in righteousness, justice, and equity;

4 to give prudence to the simple, knowledge and discretion to the young man:

5 that the wise man may hear, and increase in learning; that the man of understanding may attain to sound counsel:

6 to understand a proverb, and parables, the words and riddles of the wise.

7 The fear of Yahweh is the beginning of knowledge; but the foolish despise wisdom and instruction.

The Enticement of Sin

8 My son, listen to your father's instruction, and don't forsake your mother's teaching

9 for they will be a garland to grace your head, and chains around your neck.

10 My son, if sinners entice you, don't consent.

11 If they say, "Come with us, Let's lay in wait for blood; let's lurk secretly for the innocent without cause;

12 let's swallow them up alive like Sheol, and whole, like those who go down into the pit.

13 We'll find all valuable wealth. We'll fill our houses with spoil.

14 You shall cast your lot among us. We'll all have one purse.

15 My son, don't walk in the way with them. Keep your foot from their path

16 for their feet run to evil. They hurry to shed blood

17 For in vain is the net spread in the sight of any bird

18 but these lay wait for their own blood. They lurk secretly for their own lives

19 So are the ways of everyone who is greedy for gain. It takes away the life of its owners

Wisdom Calls Out Publicly

20 Wisdom calls aloud in the street. She utters her voice in the public squares.

21 She calls at the head of noisy places. At the entrance of the city gates, she utters her words:

22 "How long, you simple ones, will you love simplicity? How long will mockers delight themselves in mockery, and fools hate knowledge?

23 Turn at my reproof. Behold, I will pour out my spirit on you. I will make known my words to you.

24 Because I have called, and you have refused; I have stretched out my hand, and no one has paid attention;

25 but you have ignored all my counsel, and wanted none of my reproof;

26 I also will laugh at your disaster. I will mock when calamity overtakes you;

27 when calamity overtakes you like a storm, when your disaster comes on like a whirlwind; when distress and anguish come on you.

28 Then will they call on me, but I will not answer. They will seek me diligently, but they will not find me;

29 because they hated knowledge, and didn't choose the fear of Yahweh.

30 They wanted none of my counsel. They despised all my reproof.

31 Therefore they will eat of the fruit of their own way, and be filled with their own schemes.

32 For the backsliding of the simple will kill them. The careless ease of fools will destroy them.

33 But whoever listens to me will dwell securely, and will be at ease, without fear of harm."

Thoughts to Reflect Upon:

Why is godly wisdom so important? How does Proverbs 1 set the tone for the rest of the book? What is healthy vs. unhealthy fear? How can you focus on making your fear productive? Why must the Lord be the primary source of wisdom in our lives?

Verse of the Day: 01/   Date:

_____
_____
_____

Journal/Notes Section-

_____
_____
_____
_____
_____
_____
_____
_____
_____
_____
_____
_____
_____
_____

Proverbs 2: Flee from Immorality

It is when we pursue knowledge that God gives us the wisdom to understand what the fear of the Lord is. God continually shows the upright in heart how to walk by acting as a shield to those who uphold integrity, righteousness, and justice. The more we gain an understanding of God's word, the greater our ability to discern right from wrong and to steer away from the crooked, the devious, the immoral, and all those who enjoy the things of darkness.

How do we pursue knowledge? By investing richly in God's Word. It's crucial that we make reading the Bible a daily practice in our lives. Through the Bible, God reveals to us the truth about Him, ourselves, and the world in which we live. Not only that, but He also reveals the divine purpose He has prepared for our lives. The knowledge we find throughout God's Word is essential for every aspect of our daily lives.

Without this daily practice, it is extremely difficult, if not impossible, to discern God's Will for our lives. There are also times in life when it is challenging to determine what is right or wrong in a given situation. But when armed with the wisdom we find within the pages of the Bible, we are able to draw on God's wisdom, which is limitless in comparison to our own.

The knowledge and wisdom we gain from God's Word will protect us from immorality, which only leads to ruin. Instead, we will be clothed in the holiness and righteousness of Christ, leading us to live lives pleasing to God.

Proverbs 2: Scripture

The Benefits of Wisdom

1 My son, if you will receive my words, and store up my commandments within you;

2 So as to turn your ear to wisdom, and apply your heart to understanding;

3 Yes, if you call out for discernment, and lift up your voice for understanding;

4 If you seek her as silver, and search for her as for hidden treasures:

5 then you will understand the fear of Yahweh, and find the knowledge of God.

6 For Yahweh gives wisdom. Out of his mouth comes knowledge and understanding.

7 He lays up sound wisdom for the upright. He is a shield to those who walk in integrity;

8 that he may guard the paths of justice, and preserve the way of his saints.

9 Then you will understand righteousness and justice, equity and every good path.

10 For wisdom will enter into your heart. Knowledge will be pleasant to your soul.

11 Discretion will watch over you. Understanding will keep you,

12 to deliver you from the way of evil, from the men who speak perverse things;

13 who forsake the paths of uprightness, to walk in the ways of darkness;

14 who rejoice to do evil, and delight in the perverseness of evil;

15 who are crooked in their ways, and wayward in their paths:

Immorality Brings Disaster

16 To deliver you from the strange woman, even from the foreigner who flatters with her words;

17 who forsakes the friend of her youth, and forgets the covenant of her God:

18 for her house leads down to death, her paths to the dead.

19 None who go to her return again, neither do they attain to the paths of life:

20 that you may walk in the way of good men, and keep the paths of the righteous.

21 For the upright will dwell in the land. The perfect will remain in it.

22 But the wicked will be cut off from the land. The treacherous will be rooted out of it.

Thoughts to Reflect Upon:

How does godly wisdom bless us with the Lord's protection? How does the Bible teach us right from wrong? How does that put us in right standing with God? What does it mean to pursue knowledge? How can you make Bible reading a daily part of your life?

Verse of the Day: 02/   Date:

_____
_____
_____

Journal/Notes Section-

_____
_____
_____
_____
_____
_____
_____
_____
_____
_____
_____
_____
_____
_____
_____
_____
_____
_____
_____

Proverbs 3: Trust in the Lord with All Your Heart

This chapter addresses the reader as "My son." This form of address could mean Solomon was writing to his own son; however, it was common for teachers to include students in a father-son relationship. That includes us! The point is that this instruction is imparted in a loving, fatherly way and not as a set of marching orders. The key verse is to trust in Yahweh with all our heart and not lean on our own understanding, for with God's wisdom, we tap into His creative power and His blessings of long life, health, security, peace, and prosperity. When God's commandments rule our hearts, His mercy and truth will shine through us. As we honor God too with our giving, we can be assured of abundance. Yahweh blesses the righteous but brings shame upon fools.

We live in a world that often operates in direct opposition to the ways of God. That reality makes it very challenging to live righteous lives under Christ. The world is turning in one direction, and we are called to walk the other way! How are we to accomplish this?

The answer is simple: by heeding Solomon's instruction to look toward God's direction instead of leaning on our own understanding. Our human perspective and understanding are limited and fleeting, but God's is boundless. Not only that, but He is our Father who loves us more than we could ever comprehend. For those reasons, and so many more, we can trust Him to guide the direction of our lives.

Solomon encourages us out of love to trust in the Lord. Trusting in the Lord means having full confidence in His direction for your life. Commit your future into the hands of God today. He will lead you to the fullness of your potential in Christ.

Proverbs 3: Scripture

Trust in the Lord

1 My son, don't forget my teaching; but let your heart keep my commandments:

2 for length of days, and years of life, and peace, will they add to you.

3 Don't let kindness and truth forsake you. Bind them around your neck. Write them on the tablet of your heart.

4 So you will find favor, and good understanding in the sight of God and man.

5 Trust in Yahweh with all your heart, and don't lean on your own understanding.

6 In all your ways acknowledge him, and he will make your paths straight.

7 Don't be wise in your own eyes. Fear Yahweh, and depart from evil.

8 It will be health to your body, and nourishment to your bones.

9 Honor Yahweh with your substance, with the first fruits of all your increase:

10 so your barns will be filled with plenty, and your vats will overflow with new wine.

11 My son, don't despise Yahweh's discipline, neither be weary of his reproof:

12 for whom Yahweh loves, he reproves; even as a father reproves the son in whom he delights.

Blessed is he Who Finds Wisdom

13 Happy is the man who finds wisdom, the man who gets understanding.

14 For her good profit is better than getting silver, and her return is better than fine gold.

15 She is more precious than rubies. None of the things you can desire are to be compared to her.

16 Length of days is in her right hand. In her left hand are riches and honor.

17 Her ways are ways of pleasantness. All her paths are peace.

18 She is a tree of life to those who lay hold of her. Happy is everyone who retains her.

19 By wisdom Yahweh founded the earth. By understanding, he established the heavens.

20 By his knowledge, the depths were broken up, and the skies drop down the dew.

21 My son, let them not depart from your eyes. Keep sound wisdom and discretion:

22 so they will be life to your soul, and grace for your neck.

23 Then you shall walk in your way securely. Your foot won't stumble.

24 When you lie down, you will not be afraid. Yes, you will lie down, and your sleep will be sweet.

25 Don't be afraid of sudden fear, neither of the desolation of the wicked, when it comes:

26 for Yahweh will be your confidence, and will keep your foot from being taken.

27 Don't withhold good from those to whom it is due, when it is in the power of your hand to do it.

28 Don't say to your neighbor, "Go, and come again; tomorrow I will give it to you," when you have it by you.

29 Don't devise evil against your neighbor, since he dwells securely by you.

30 Don't strive with a man without cause, if he has done you no harm.

31 Don't envy the man of violence. Choose none of his ways.

32 For the perverse is an abomination to Yahweh, but his friendship is with the upright.

33 Yahweh's curse is in the house of the wicked, but he blesses the habitation of the righteous.

34 Surely he mocks the mockers, but he gives grace to the humble.

35 The wise will inherit glory, but shame will be the promotion of fools.

Thoughts to Reflect Upon:

Why is giving important? How does it reflect the heart of God? How are we to live when the world is often in direct conflict with God's teachings? What does it mean to be set apart for the Lord? Why does God's wisdom ALWAYS trump human understanding? How does following Him unlock our true potential?

Verse of the Day: 03/   Date:

_____
_____
_____

Journal/Notes Section-

_____
_____
_____
_____
_____
_____
_____
_____
_____
_____
_____
_____
_____
_____
_____
_____
_____
_____

Proverbs 4:
A Father's Instruction

Listen, sons, to a father's instruction. Once again, we are to LISTEN. As children, we adore our parents and treasure their advice like gold. Similarly, in all our seeking, God advises us to get wisdom, which is the most precious thing. By following God's wisdom, we put ourselves on "the path of the righteous" and become like the "dawning light that shines more and more." We avoid the way of evil and put corrupt speech far from us. Above all, we should guard our heart (our core being), for out of it come the springs of life.

Most of us haven't ever learned what it truly means to be a good listener. Jesus often said before teaching, "Whoever has ears to hear, let him hear!" (Mark 4:9). What did He mean by this curious expression?

Jesus had been experiencing in His ministry that a lot of people were not comprehending the truth that He was trying to reveal to them. It was probably a bit frustrating because what He was trying to tell them wasn't complicated at all! But the people still asked questions as if they had no understanding.

Have you ever had a situation where you were attempting to explain something simple to someone and it became very difficult because they were not listening carefully enough to understand? That's exactly what was going on here. The people were so blinded by their expectations, previous experiences, and personal motivations that they were not actually paying attention to the words that Jesus was saying.

When we are listening to the voice of Jesus in our lives, we must ensure that we are good listeners. The truth that He is trying to pour into our lives is irreplaceable for our spiritual health. Without it, we can never live lives pleasing to God, nor can we guard our hearts in the process.

Proverbs Chapter 4: Scripture

Listen to a Father's Instruction

1 Listen, sons, to a father's instruction. Pay attention and know understanding;

2 for I give you sound learning. Don't forsake my law.

3 For I was a son to my father, tender and an only child in the sight of my mother.

4 He taught me, and said to me: "Let your heart retain my words. Keep my commandments, and live.

5 Get wisdom. Get understanding. Don't forget, neither swerve from the words of my mouth.

6 Don't forsake her, and she will preserve you. Love her, and she will keep you.

7 Wisdom is supreme. Get wisdom. Yes, though it costs all your possessions, get understanding.

8 Esteem her, and she will exalt you. She will bring you to honor, when you embrace her.

9 She will give to your head a garland of grace. She will deliver a crown of splendor to you."

10 Listen, my son, and receive my sayings. The years of your life will be many.

11 I have taught you in the way of wisdom. I have led you in straight paths.

12 When you go, your steps will not be hampered. When you run, you will not stumble.

13 Take firm hold of instruction. Don't let her go. Keep her, for she is your life.

14 Don't enter into the path of the wicked. Don't walk in the way of evil men.

15 Avoid it, and don't pass by it. Turn from it, and pass on.

16 For they don't sleep, unless they do evil. Their sleep is taken away, unless they make someone fall.

17 For they eat the bread of wickedness, and drink the wine of violence.

18 But the path of the righteous is like the dawning light, that shines more and more until the perfect day.

19 The way of the wicked is like darkness. They don't know what they stumble over.

20 My son, attend to my words. Turn your ear to my sayings.

21 Let them not depart from your eyes. Keep them in the midst of your heart.

22 For they are life to those who find them, and health to their whole body.

23 Keep your heart with all diligence, for out of it is the wellspring of life.

24 Put away from yourself a perverse mouth. Put corrupt lips far from you.

25 Let your eyes look straight ahead. Fix your gaze directly before you.

26 Make the path of your feet level. Let all of your ways be established.

27 Don't turn to the right hand nor to the left. Remove your foot from evil.

Thoughts to Reflect Upon:

Why is listening so important? Why can it be so hard? How can we work on being better listeners and applying the truth that Jesus presents to us? What does it mean when Proverbs 4:23 calls our heart "the wellspring of life"? Why is it so crucial that we guard our hearts diligently? How does God help us to accomplish this?

Verse of the Day: 04/   Date:

_____
_____
_____

Journal/Notes Section-

_____
_____
_____
_____
_____
_____
_____
_____
_____
_____
_____
_____
_____
_____
_____
_____
_____

Proverbs 5: Cherish Faithfulness

Solomon warns us not to be deceived by sexual enticements or suffer severe consequences. The seductress is depicted as a woman, but the message can also be a warning to a woman not to fall into temptation herself. Men are charmed by beauty, women by flattery, as the smooth-talking charmer lures them on a path straight to death. Of what value are the fleeting pleasures of sin when they inevitably lead to destruction?

On the other hand, staying faithful in marriage, always captivated by the love of one's youth, will bring joy and happiness. If we are to forsake the covenant of marriage, we are reminded that "the ways of man are before Yahweh's eyes. He examines all his paths." Solomon warns us that we will ultimately regret our folly.

God has created love, marriage, and sexual intimacy to be beautiful and life-giving to us. His design is not intended to limit us or control us, but rather lead us to the fullness of all of these things! God wants us to experience all that love, marriage, and intimacy have to offer, and that's why He teaches us to treat them all with holiness and respect.

When we indulge in these pleasures outside of their proper place and time, we are simply robbing ourselves of their true purpose. We are merely accepting a cheap, shallow version because we have not waited for the right time. Not only does this rob us in the present, but it creates significant hurdles and pain when we do enter into the holy covenant of marriage.

That's why it is essential that we develop a healthy and godly understanding of love, sex, and marriage. It is a great challenge to resist temptation in most of our lives, but God's wisdom will equip us with everything we need to live the romantic side of our lives according to God's design.

Proverbs 5: Scripture

Avoid Immorality

My son, pay attention to my wisdom.
  Turn your ear to my understanding,
2 that you may maintain discretion,
  that your lips may preserve knowledge.
3 For the lips of an adulteress drip honey.
  Her mouth is smoother than oil,
4 but in the end she is as bitter as wormwood,
  and as sharp as a two-edged sword.
5 Her feet go down to death.
  Her steps lead straight to Sheol.
6 She gives no thought to the way of life.
  Her ways are crooked, and she doesn't know it.

7 Now therefore, my sons, listen to me.
  Don't depart from the words of my mouth.
8 Remove your way far from her.
  Don't come near the door of her house,
9 lest you give your honor to others,
  and your years to the cruel one;
10 lest strangers feast on your wealth,
  and your labors enrich another man's house.
11 You will groan at your latter end,
  when your flesh and your body are consumed,
12 and say, "How I have hated instruction,
  and my heart despised reproof.
13 I haven't obeyed the voice of my teachers,
  nor turned my ear to those who instructed me!

14 I have come to the brink of utter ruin,
   among the gathered assembly."

15 Drink water out of your own cistern,
   running water out of your own well.
16 Should your springs overflow in the streets,
   streams of water in the public squares?
17 Let them be for yourself alone,
   not for strangers with you.
18 Let your spring be blessed.
   Rejoice in the wife of your youth.
19 A loving doe and a graceful deer—
   let her breasts satisfy you at all times.
   Be captivated always with her love.
20 For why should you, my son, be captivated with an adulteress?
   Why embrace the bosom of another?
21 For the ways of man are before Yahweh's eyes.
   He examines all his paths.
22 The evil deeds of the wicked ensnare him.
   The cords of his sin hold him firmly.
23 He will die for lack of instruction.
   In the greatness of his folly, he will go astray.

Thoughts to Reflect Upon:

Why does the Bible take marriage so seriously? What is God's vision for marriage compared to that of the world? Why are sexual sins so destructive in one's life? How can we avoid them? How can you develop a healthy view of love, sex, and marriage? How will that worldview shape your life?

Verse of the Day: 05/   Date:

_____
_____
_____

Journal/Notes Section-

_____
_____
_____
_____
_____
_____
_____
_____
_____
_____
_____
_____
_____
_____
_____
_____
_____
_____
_____

Proverbs 6: The Folly of Indiscretion

Here is good practical advice from never becoming a guarantor in financial transactions to having a good work ethic. Be like the ant who stocks up for the future. If you're like the sluggard or lazy person, you will experience great hardship, as poverty will come upon you without warning.

This is a powerful reminder that God's wisdom helps us in every aspect of our lives. For many, matters of finance don't seem like the "spiritual things" that the Bible would want to teach about. But God does indeed desire to be an inseparable part of our lives in every way, including our finances. Never limit the Bible's ability to speak into whatever situations you experience in life.

Solomon also has harsh words for the person with a loose tongue who slanders his neighbor, devises evil, and continually sows discord. These actions are among the things the Lord hates: arrogance, lying, murder, scheming, mischief-making, and bearing false witness.

The Bible holds no punches when it comes to the power of our words and the responsibility we have to speak words that build people up instead of tearing them down. Through our words, we have the ability to either hurt or heal. It's something we can't take lightly! Commit to always speaking words of love and encouragement to everyone in your life.

Solomon reiterates the warnings about casual sex. This will cause the offender to squander their wealth, lose their reputation, and incur the wrath of the wronged spouse. There is no excuse for this kind of behavior, and it flies directly in the face of God's design for our lives.

Proverbs 6: Scripture

Warnings against Foolishness

My son, if you have become collateral for your neighbor,
  if you have struck your hands in pledge for a stranger,
2 you are trapped by the words of your mouth;
  you are ensnared with the words of your mouth.
3 Do this now, my son, and deliver yourself,
  since you have come into the hand of your neighbor.
Go, humble yourself.
  Press your plea with your neighbor.
4 Give no sleep to your eyes,
  nor slumber to your eyelids.
5 Free yourself, like a gazelle from the hand of the hunter,
  like a bird from the snare of the fowler.
6 Go to the ant, you sluggard.
  Consider her ways, and be wise;
7 which having no chief, overseer, or ruler,
8   provides her bread in the summer,
  and gathers her food in the harvest.
9 How long will you sleep, sluggard?
  When will you arise out of your sleep?
10 A little sleep, a little slumber,
  a little folding of the hands to sleep:
11 so your poverty will come as a robber,
  and your scarcity as an armed man.
12 A worthless person, a man of iniquity,
  is he who walks with a perverse mouth,
13 who winks with his eyes, who signals with his feet,

who motions with his fingers,
14 in whose heart is perverseness,
   who devises evil continually,
   who always sows discord.
15 Therefore his calamity will come suddenly.
   He will be broken suddenly, and that without remedy.
16 There are six things which Yahweh hates;
   yes, seven which are an abomination to him:
17 arrogant eyes, a lying tongue,
   hands that shed innocent blood,
18 a heart that devises wicked schemes,
   feet that are swift in running to mischief,
19 a false witness who utters lies,
   and he who sows discord among brothers.

Warnings against Adultery

20 My son, keep your father's commandment,
   and don't forsake your mother's teaching.
21 Bind them continually on your heart.
   Tie them around your neck.
22 When you walk, it will lead you.
   When you sleep, it will watch over you.
   When you awake, it will talk with you.
23 For the commandment is a lamp,
   and the law is light.
   Reproofs of instruction are the way of life,
24 to keep you from the immoral woman,
   from the flattery of the wayward wife's tongue.
25 Don't lust after her beauty in your heart,
   neither let her captivate you with her eyelids.
26 For a prostitute reduces you to a piece of bread.
   The adulteress hunts for your precious life.
27 Can a man scoop fire into his lap,
   and his clothes not be burned?

28 Or can one walk on hot coals,
   and his feet not be scorched?
29 So is he who goes into his neighbor's wife.
   Whoever touches her will not be unpunished.
30 Men don't despise a thief
   if he steals to satisfy himself when he is hungry;
31 but if he is found, he shall restore seven times.
   He shall give all the wealth of his house.
32 He who commits adultery with a woman is void of understanding.
   He who does it destroys his own soul.
33 He will get wounds and dishonor.
   His reproach will not be wiped away.
34 For jealousy arouses the fury of the husband.
   He won't spare in the day of vengeance.
35 He won't regard any ransom,
   neither will he rest content, though you give many gifts.

Thoughts to Reflect Upon:

Why is it important to have a strong work ethic? Why is it important to make wise financial decisions? How does God speak into our finances? How is money a "spiritual thing"? Why do our words hold so much power? How can we ensure that we are using them for good and not to tear others down?

Verse of the Day: 06/   Date:

_____
_____
_____

Journal/Notes Section-

_____
_____
_____
_____
_____
_____
_____
_____
_____
_____
_____
_____
_____
_____
_____
_____
_____
_____
_____

Proverbs 7: Warning against Adultery

Solomon admonishes the reader in a fatherly way to keep God's commandments within him. God tells us, "Keep my commandments and live," for God's wisdom is the way of life. We are to hold onto life's precious pearls of wisdom so that we may live abundantly in Christ.

It's easy to do our daily Bible reading and/or devotional, feel inspired in the moment, then go about our lives in a routine way. But it's essential that we take the wisdom we have gained and carry it with us throughout our day, finding places to apply it.

If we aren't actually living out the things we are learning through Christ, our faith is fruitless in our lives! In that case, we will become like the Pharisees, who knew a lot about the Bible but failed continually at actually applying it to their lives correctly. It's critical that we not only discern the Will of God, but also that we live it out.

This chapter also further extends the warning against adultery, and we see that the tactics of the prostitute haven't changed much. She is deceptive and dangerous. She stalks her young man like a predator, and with flattering lips and enticements, she seduces him. Little does the ignorant man realize that this moment of pleasure will ultimately cost him his life.

This is often how sexual sin happens in our lives. We are continually tempted and overcome by our desires, sometimes seemingly out of nowhere. That's why it is crucial that we constantly guard our hearts against such advances, commit wholly to purity, and live out our sexual lives in accordance with God's design.

Proverbs 7: Scripture

Warnings about the Adulteress

My son, keep my words.
   Lay up my commandments within you.
2 Keep my commandments and live!
   Guard my teaching as the apple of your eye.
3 Bind them on your fingers.
   Write them on the tablet of your heart.
4 Tell wisdom, "You are my sister."
   Call understanding your relative,
5 that they may keep you from the strange woman,
   from the foreigner who flatters with her words.
6 For at the window of my house,
   I looked out through my lattice.
7 I saw among the simple ones.
   I discerned among the youths a young man void of understanding,
8 passing through the street near her corner,
   he went the way to her house,
9 in the twilight, in the evening of the day,
   in the middle of the night and in the darkness.
10 Behold, there a woman met him with the attire of a prostitute,
   and with crafty intent.
11 She is loud and defiant.
   Her feet don't stay in her house.
12 Now she is in the streets, now in the squares,
   and lurking at every corner.
13 So she caught him, and kissed him.
   With an impudent face she said to him:
14 "Sacrifices of peace offerings are with me.
   Today I have paid my vows.
15 Therefore I came out to meet you,
   to diligently seek your face,

and I have found you.
16 I have spread my couch with carpets of tapestry,
   with striped cloths of the yarn of Egypt.
17 I have perfumed my bed with myrrh, aloes, and cinnamon.
18 Come, let's take our fill of loving until the morning.
   Let's solace ourselves with loving.
19 For my husband isn't at home.
   He has gone on a long journey.
20 He has taken a bag of money with him.
   He will come home at the full moon."
21 With persuasive words, she led him astray.
   With the flattering of her lips, she seduced him.
22 He followed her immediately,
   as an ox goes to the slaughter,
   as a fool stepping into a noose.
23 Until an arrow strikes through his liver,
   as a bird hurries to the snare,
   and doesn't know that it will cost his life.
24 Now therefore, sons, listen to me.
   Pay attention to the words of my mouth.
25 Don't let your heart turn to her ways.
   Don't go astray in her paths,
26 for she has thrown down many wounded.
   Yes, all her slain are a mighty army.
27 Her house is the way to Sheol,
   going down to the rooms of death.

Thoughts to Reflect Upon:

Why must God's teachings be the foundation for our lives? How do Christ's teachings lead to abundance in every aspect of our lives? How can we ensure that our faith is bearing fruit? Why is adultery so dangerous? How does it destroy God's vision for healthy relationships?

Verse of the Day: 07/   Date:

___

Journal/Notes Section-

Proverbs 8: Wisdom Calls from on High

Anyone willing to listen can obtain wisdom, for wisdom makes herself visible to all. "Does not wisdom call? Does not understanding raise her voice?" Wisdom is not hard to access at all, and it is intended for everyone. Everyone has the wisdom to do what is right by ignoring the temptation of sin. "Wickedness is an abomination to my lips," says Solomon.

A person who chooses to follow wisdom may not have many material possessions. Still, they will be better off than a rich man, for wisdom is indeed more precious than silver and gold. Wisdom is inherent in the nature of God and was already there at the creation of the world, "Rejoicing in his whole world. My delight was with the sons of men."

Don't we all want to better ourselves, be healthier, and attain the next level in our lives? Yes, we are all in search of wisdom. Sadly, we are often looking for it in the wrong places when the true answer is right in front of us.

All the wisdom we need to achieve greatness in every area of our lives is found in God's Word. God doesn't withhold any wisdom from us, nor does He make it difficult for us to find. It's right there, waiting for us to learn from it and apply it in our lives!

So, in reality, we are the only ones holding back on this gracious invitation to receive. It's time for us to invest richly in God's Word and drink deeply of the knowledge it has to give. The best way to do this is to commit to a daily Bible reading plan, taking what you learn each day and applying it to your life.

When you do, you will grow in ways you could never imagine. Righteousness will fill your life and lead you to the fullness of the potential God has placed within you!

Proverbs 8: Scripture

The Excellence of Wisdom

1 Doesn't wisdom cry out? Doesn't understanding raise her voice?

2 On the top of high places by the way, Where the paths meet, she stands.

3 Beside the gates, at the entry of the city, At the entry doors, she cries aloud:

4 "To you men, I call! I send my voice to the sons of mankind.

5 You simple, understand prudence. You fools, be of an understanding heart.

6 Hear, for I will speak excellent things. The opening of my lips is for right things.

7 For my mouth speaks truth. Wickedness is an abomination to my lips.

8 All the words of my mouth are in righteousness. There is nothing crooked or perverse in them.

9 They are all plain to him who understands, Right to those who find knowledge.

10 Receive my instruction rather than silver; Knowledge rather than choice gold.

11 For wisdom is better than rubies. All the things that may be desired can't be compared to it.

12 "I, wisdom, have made prudence my dwelling. Find out knowledge and discretion.

13 The fear of Yahweh is to hate evil. I hate pride, arrogance, the evil way, and the perverse mouth.

14 Counsel and sound knowledge are mine. I have understanding and power.

15 By me kings reign, And princes decree justice.

16 By me princes rule; Nobles, and all the righteous rulers of the earth.

17 I love those who love me. Those who seek me diligently will find me.

18 With me are riches, honor, Enduring wealth, and prosperity.

19 My fruit is better than gold, yes, than fine gold; My yield than choice silver.

20 I walk in the way of righteousness, In the midst of the paths of justice;

21 That I may give wealth to those who love me. I fill their treasuries.

22 "Yahweh possessed me in the beginning of his work, Before his deeds of old.

23 I was set up from everlasting, from the beginning, Before the earth existed.

24 When there were no depths, I was brought forth, When there were no springs abounding with water.

25 Before the mountains were settled in place, Before the hills, I was brought forth;

26 While as yet he had not made the earth, nor the fields, Nor the beginning of the dust of the world.

27 When he established the heavens, I was there; When he set a circle on the surface of the deep,

28 When he established the clouds above, When the springs of the deep became strong,

29 When he gave to the sea its boundary, That the waters should not violate his commandment, When he marked out the foundations of the earth;

30 Then I was the craftsman by his side. I was a delight day by day, Always rejoicing before him,

31 Rejoicing in his whole world. My delight was with the sons of men.

32 "Now therefore, my sons, listen to me, For blessed are those who keep my ways.

33 Hear instruction, and be wise, Don't refuse it.

34 Blessed is the man who hears me, Watching daily at my gates, Waiting at my door posts.

35 For whoever finds me, finds life, And will obtain favor from Yahweh.

36 But he who sins against me wrongs his own soul. All those who hate me love death."

Thoughts to Reflect Upon:

How does God make wisdom available to all? Why is it crucial that we answer wisdom's call? How does godly wisdom lead us away from sin and bless us with abundant life? What does it mean to rejoice in the Word of God?

Verse of the Day: 08/   Date:

_____
_____
_____

Journal/Notes Section-

_____
_____
_____
_____
_____
_____
_____
_____
_____
_____
_____
_____
_____
_____
_____
_____
_____
_____
_____
_____

Proverbs 9: Folly Shouts Out

The writer repeats his core teaching: "The fear of Yahweh is the beginning of wisdom." By obeying God and seeking wisdom, we are on the path to godly character and righteous living.

There is a sharp distinction between godly and worldly wisdom, and both are equally vocal. Godly wisdom calls out from the high places to the foolish, "Leave your simple ways, and live. Walk in the way of understanding." At the same time, foolishness shouts out to passers-by, also from a seat "in the high places of the city" to see whom she can ensnare. She is "loud, undisciplined, and knows nothing," yet the simple go to her, unaware that they are joining the company of the dead.

In imparting wisdom, we should be discerning whom we decide to correct and not cast our pearls before swine. If someone does not listen, let's not waste our time. While we can follow God's call to spread HIS love and wisdom to the ends of the Earth, we can't make everyone listen. You can never wake up someone who pretends to be asleep. There are times we will have to move on, because ultimately they are the ones to decide if they will apply what we have taught them or not!

All we truly have control of is living out God's truth in our own lives and following His call upon our hearts. If we do those two things, we can be assured that we are living in alignment with His Will. The Holy Spirit will take care of the rest and make us powerful ambassadors of God's Kingdom.

Proverbs 9: Scripture

The Way of Wisdom

1 Wisdom has built her house. She has carved out her seven pillars.

2 She has prepared her meat. She has mixed her wine. She has also set her table.

3 She has sent out her maidens. She cries from the highest places of the city:

4 "Whoever is simple, let him turn in here!" As for him who is void of understanding, she says to him,

5 "Come, eat some of my bread, Drink some of the wine which I have mixed!

6 Leave your simple ways, and live. Walk in the way of understanding."

7 He who corrects a mocker invites insult. He who reproves a wicked man invites abuse.

8 Don't reprove a scoffer, lest he hate you. Reprove a wise man, and he will love you.

9 Instruct a wise man, and he will be still wiser. Teach a righteous man, and he will increase in learning.

10 The fear of Yahweh is the beginning of wisdom. The knowledge of the Holy One is understanding.

11 For by me your days will be multiplied. The years of your life will be increased.

12 If you are wise, you are wise for yourself. If you mock, you alone will bear it.

The Way of Folly

13 The foolish woman is loud, Undisciplined, and knows nothing.

14 She sits at the door of her house, On a seat in the high places of the city,

15 To call to those who pass by, who go straight on their ways,

16 "Whoever is simple, let him turn in here." As for him who is void of understanding, she says to him,

17 "Stolen water is sweet. Food eaten in secret is pleasant."

18 But he doesn't know that the dead are there, that her guests are in the depths of Sheol.

Thoughts to Reflect Upon:

How does obeying God produce godly character in our lives? How is God's wisdom different from that of the world? Which is governing your life? How can we live out God's wisdom in our lives? How does the Holy Spirit aid us in this endeavor?

Verse of the Day: 09/   Date:

_____
_____
_____

Journal/Notes Section-

_____
_____
_____
_____
_____
_____
_____
_____
_____
_____
_____
_____
_____
_____
_____
_____
_____
_____

Proverbs 10: Two Paths – Righteous vs. Wicked

Here, we have a series of contrasts between the way of the righteous and the path of the wicked. This contrast hinges on the word "but." One leads to life and the other death. The wise in heart accept God's commandments and walk blamelessly with discernment, working diligently and guarding their tongue. Though they make mistakes, they are open to correction. By contrast, the wicked scoff at correction and harbor violence in their heart and their words. The cost of not listening to the voice of wisdom is not worth the promises of the enemy. Living a life of righteousness brings many rewards, and in the final analysis, "When the whirlwind passes, the wicked is no more, but the righteous stand firm forever."

While it's one thing to read about the differences between righteousness and wickedness in the Bible, it's another to be able to recognize this very real tug-of-war in our own lives. Evil is real and a constant threat. Satan will stoop to any low in an attempt to pull us away from our relationship with the Lord.

That's why we must understand the seriousness of wickedness in this world and learn what it means to truly live righteous lives. Then, we can live the kind of life that naturally fends off the advances of our enemy and continually builds up faith within us.

Meditate and pray on the differences between righteousness and wickedness in our world. Ask that God would clearly show you the fine line between them as you live out your life.

Proverbs 10: Scripture

Solomon's Proverbs: The Wise Son

1 The proverbs of Solomon. A wise son makes a glad father; but a foolish son brings grief to his mother.

2 Treasures of wickedness profit nothing, but righteousness delivers from death.

3 Yahweh will not allow the soul of the righteous to go hungry, but he thrusts away the desire of the wicked.

4 He becomes poor who works with a lazy hand, but the hand of the diligent brings wealth.

5 He who gathers in summer is a wise son, but he who sleeps during the harvest is a son who causes shame.

6 Blessings are on the head of the righteous, but violence covers the mouth of the wicked.

7 The memory of the righteous is blessed, but the name of the wicked will rot.

8 The wise in heart accept commandments, but a chattering fool will fall.

9 He who walks blamelessly walks surely, but he who perverts his ways will be found out.

10 One winking with the eye causes sorrow, but a chattering fool will fall.

11 The mouth of the righteous is a spring of life, but violence covers the mouth of the wicked.

12 Hatred stirs up strife, but love covers all wrongs.

13 Wisdom is found on the lips of him who has discernment, but a rod is for the back of him who is void of understanding.

14 Wise men lay up knowledge, but the mouth of the foolish is near ruin.

15 The rich man's wealth is his strong city. The destruction of the poor is their poverty.

16 The labor of the righteous leads to life. The increase of the wicked leads to sin.

17 He is in the way of life who heeds correction, but he who forsakes reproof leads others astray.

18 He who hides hatred has lying lips. He who utters a slander is a fool.

19 In the multitude of words there is no lack of disobedience, but he who restrains his lips does wisely.

20 The tongue of the righteous is like choice silver. The heart of the wicked is of little worth.

21 The lips of the righteous feed many, but the foolish die for lack of understanding.

22 Yahweh's blessing brings wealth, and he adds no trouble to it.

23 It is a fool's pleasure to do wickedness, but wisdom is a man of understanding's pleasure.

24 What the wicked fear, will overtake them, but the desire of the righteous will be granted.

25 When the whirlwind passes, the wicked is no more, but the righteous stand firm forever.

26 As vinegar to the teeth, and as smoke to the eyes, so is the sluggard to those who send him.

27 The fear of Yahweh prolongs days, but the years of the wicked shall be shortened.

28 The prospect of the righteous is joy, but the hope of the wicked will perish.

29 The way of Yahweh is a stronghold to the upright, but it is a destruction to the workers of iniquity.

30 The righteous will never be removed, but the wicked will not dwell in the land.

31 The mouth of the righteous brings forth wisdom, but the perverse tongue will be cut off.

32 The lips of the righteous know what is acceptable, but the mouth of the wicked is perverse.

Thoughts to Reflect Upon:

Does this chapter show you clearly the difference between the path of the righteous and the path of the wicked? Which are you on? Why is living righteously crucial to abundant life and a relationship with God? How can you ensure you're on the right path?

Verse of the Day:10/   Date:

_____
_____
_____

Journal/Notes Section-

_____
_____
_____
_____
_____
_____
_____
_____
_____
_____
_____
_____
_____
_____
_____
_____
_____
_____

Proverbs 11:
The Fruit of Righteous Living

God loves honesty and abhors cheating. We are called to serve others, be humble, act with integrity, and be wise in our dealings with others. When we are obedient to wisdom and truth, a blessing is bestowed upon us. And when we are blessed, so is the entire community: "By the blessing of the upright, the city is exalted, but it is overthrown by the mouth of the wicked." Moreover, in the godly counsel of the upright, the nation enjoys victory.

God loves a cheerful giver, and a wise man does not withhold offering part of his earnings to the Lord—and that includes the needy. "Whoever brings blessings will be enriched, and one who waters will himself be watered."

This is one of the most powerful lessons we can learn throughout the Scriptures. The way we live our lives affects others. You must ask yourself the question: Am I going to live in a way that benefits others?

God created us to all be connected. Just as God is eternally relational through the beautiful mystery of the Holy Trinity, we too made in His image are relational. Because of this design, when we serve others, we grow according to God's purpose for us!

Honestly evaluate how you handle your relationships. Are you being honest and serving others to the best of your ability and according to your God-given gifts? Remember, the Lord blesses and honors an honest heart. If you desire to grow in faith, you must focus on serving others, just as Jesus did.

Proverbs 11: Scripture

A False Balance is an Abomination

1 A false balance is an abomination to Yahweh, but accurate weights are his delight.

2 When pride comes, then comes shame, but with humility comes wisdom.

3 The integrity of the upright shall guide them, but the perverseness of the treacherous shall destroy them.

4 Riches do not profit in the day of wrath, but righteousness delivers from death.

5 The righteousness of the blameless will directs his way, but the wicked shall fall by his own wickedness.

6 The righteousness of the upright shall deliver them, but the unfaithful will be trapped by evil desires.

7 When a wicked man dies, hope perishes, and expectation of power comes to nothing.

8 A righteous person is delivered out of trouble, and the wicked takes his place.

9 With his mouth the godless man destroys his neighbor, but the righteous will be delivered through knowledge.

10 When it goes well with the righteous, the city rejoices. When the wicked perish, there is shouting.

11 By the blessing of the upright, the city is exalted, but it is overthrown by the mouth of the wicked.

12 One who despises his neighbor is void of wisdom, but a man of understanding holds his peace.

13 One who brings gossip betrays a confidence, but one who is of a trustworthy spirit is one who keeps a secret.

14 Where there is no wise guidance, the nation falls, but in the multitude of counselors there is victory.

15 He who is collateral for a stranger will suffer for it, but he who refuses pledges of collateral is secure.

16 A gracious woman obtains honor, but violent men obtain riches.

17 The merciful man does good to his own soul, but he who is cruel troubles his own flesh.

18 Wicked people earn deceitful wages, but one who sows righteousness reaps a sure reward.

19 He who is truly righteous gets life. He who pursues evil gets death.

20 Those who are perverse in heart are an abomination to Yahweh, but those whose ways are blameless are his delight.

21 Most certainly, the evil man will not be unpunished, but the seed of the righteous will be delivered.

22 Like a gold ring in a pig's snout, is a beautiful woman who lacks discretion.

23 The desire of the righteous is only good. The expectation of the wicked is wrath.

24 There is one who scatters and increases yet more. There is one who withholds more than is appropriate, but gains poverty.

25 The liberal soul shall be made fat. He who waters shall be watered also himself.

26 People curse someone who withholds grain, but blessing will be on the head of him who sells it.

27 He who diligently seeks good seeks favor, but he who searches after evil, it shall come to him.

28 He who trusts in his riches will fall, but the righteous shall flourish as the green leaf.

29 He who troubles his own house shall inherit the wind. The foolish shall be servant to the wise of heart.

30 The fruit of the righteous is a tree of life. He who is wise wins souls.

31 Behold, the righteous shall be repaid in the earth, how much more the wicked and the sinner!

Thoughts to Reflect Upon:

Why are honesty and integrity so important to God? What does it mean to be a "cheerful giver"? Why does this please God? How does this reflect God's very character? How do our lives impact others? Is your life blessing others?

Verse of the Day: 11/   Date:

_____
_____
_____

Journal/Notes Section-

_____
_____
_____
_____
_____
_____
_____
_____
_____
_____
_____
_____
_____
_____
_____
_____
_____
_____
_____

Proverbs 12: Diligence and Discipline

The main teaching of Proverbs can be summed up as: "Whoever loves correction loves knowledge, but he who hates reproof is stupid." The wicked cannot stand correction and often turn against you quickly. Why is this so? Because they are proud and incapable of humbling themselves. In their minds, they are always right: "The way of a fool is right in his own eyes, but he who is wise listens to counsel."

Again, the wicked are slothful and come to poverty, while the righteous are diligent and prosper. As believers, we must love discipline and be the ones whose humility brings people to the Lord.

But what does it mean to love discipline? It means that we are eager to learn more about how we can live in way pleasing to God. It all comes down to being coachable and willing to do the work of improving ourselves on a daily basis.

As Christians, this means continually seeking out opportunities to grow in our faith. Church attendance, Bible reading, prayer, fellowship, and opportunities to serve in ministry are all great ways to establish lifelong fundamentals of a vibrant faith.

We must make a plan for our lives that will set us on a path of continual growth. Fill this list with attainable goals that will drive you forward. And, of course, do it all through faith and in collaboration with God, whose wisdom will guide you every step of your journey.

Proverbs 12: Scripture

Loving Discipline and Knowledge

1 Whoever loves correction loves knowledge, but he who hates reproof is stupid.

2 A good man shall obtain favor from Yahweh, but he will condemn a man of wicked devices.

3 A man shall not be established by wickedness, but the root of the righteous shall not be moved.

4 A worthy woman is the crown of her husband, but a disgraceful wife is as rottenness in his bones.

5 The thoughts of the righteous are just, but the advice of the wicked is deceitful.

6 The words of the wicked are about lying in wait for blood, but the speech of the upright rescues them.

7 The wicked are overthrown, and are no more, but the house of the righteous shall stand.

8 A man shall be commended according to his wisdom, but he who has a warped mind shall be despised.

9 Better is he who is lightly esteemed, and has a servant, than he who honors himself, and lacks bread.

10 A righteous man respects the life of his animal, but the tender mercies of the wicked are cruel.

11 He who tills his land shall have plenty of bread, but he who chases fantasies is void of understanding.

12 The wicked desires the plunder of evil men, but the root of the righteous flourishes.

13 An evil man is trapped by sinfulness of lips, but the righteous shall come out of trouble.

14 A man shall be satisfied with good by the fruit of his mouth. The work of a man's hands shall be rewarded to him.

15 The way of a fool is right in his own eyes, but he who is wise listens to counsel.

16 A fool shows his annoyance the same day, but one who overlooks an insult is prudent.

17 He who is truthful testifies honestly, but a false witness lies.

18 There is one who speaks rashly like the piercing of a sword, but the tongue of the wise heals.

19 Truth's lips will be established forever, but a lying tongue is only momentary.

20 Deceit is in the heart of those who plot evil, but joy comes to the promoters of peace.

21 No mischief shall happen to the righteous, but the wicked shall be filled with evil.

22 Lying lips are an abomination to Yahweh, but those who do the truth are his delight.

23 A prudent man keeps his knowledge, but the hearts of fools proclaim foolishness.

24 The hands of the diligent ones shall rule, but laziness ends in slave labor.

25 Anxiety in a man's heart weighs it down, but a kind word makes it glad.

26 A righteous person is cautious in friendship, but the way of the wicked leads them astray.

27 The slothful man doesn't roast his game, but the possessions of diligent men are prized.

28 In the way of righteousness is life; in its path there is no death.

Thoughts to Reflect Upon:

How can we see correction as a good thing? How does it help us steer clear of sin in our lives? Why is pride destructive? In contrast, how does humility enrich our lives? How does following the wisdom of God help us to remain humble in everything?

Verse of the Day: 12/   Date:

_____
_____
_____

Journal/Notes Section-

_____
_____
_____
_____
_____
_____
_____
_____
_____
_____
_____
_____
_____
_____
_____
_____
_____
_____
_____
_____

Proverbs 13: Walking with the Wise

Correction brings forth clarity to build a righteous character. As a sinner, reading Proverbs reminds me of the consequences of actions I committed in the past as a warning. "A wise son listens to his father's instruction." Just as we need to discipline our own children, God as a loving Father does not hesitate to chastise us when we go wrong. We are to take great pleasure in being corrected, even though it hurts. God also wants those who are wise to be role models for us: "One who walks with wise men grows wise," so we learn by their example and benefit from their admonitions.

Never doubt the benefits of having a spiritual mentor. God has given us fellowship as a gift through which we can find encouragement and grow in our faith. Spiritual mentors in our lives can give us a unique perspective, lift us up in faith, and hold us accountable for giving into the sins that plague our lives.

The accountability aspect cannot be overemphasized. Having someone who you can trust, who is close to you, and who knows the sin you struggle with can provide the extra strength you need to finally break through that sin that has been holding you back.

Our growth, both personally and through fellowship, must be rooted in the Lord. While there is an arsenal of self-help resources out there vying for our time and money, we must resist anything that isn't biblically sound and faith-building.

God is our Father, and He loves us more than we could ever comprehend. He is also all-knowing and all-powerful, meaning that we can trust Him in every way with the direction of our lives.

Proverbs 13: Scripture

A Wise Son Heeds His Father's Instruction

1 A wise son listens to his father's instruction, but a scoffer doesn't listen to rebuke.

2 By the fruit of his lips, a man enjoys good things; but the unfaithful crave violence.

3 He who guards his mouth guards his soul. One who opens wide his lips comes to ruin.

4 The soul of the sluggard desires, and has nothing, but the desire of the diligent shall be fully satisfied.

5 A righteous man hates lies, but a wicked man brings shame and disgrace.

6 Righteousness guards the way of integrity, but wickedness overthrows the sinner.

7 There are some who pretend to be rich, yet have nothing. There are some who pretend to be poor, yet have great wealth.

8 The ransom of a man's life is his riches, but the poor hear no threats.

9 The light of the righteous shines brightly, but the lamp of the wicked is snuffed out.

10 Pride only breeds quarrels, but with ones who take advice is wisdom.

11 Wealth gained dishonestly dwindles away, but he who gathers by hand makes it grow.

12 Hope deferred makes the heart sick, but when longing is fulfilled, it is a tree of life.

13 Whoever despises instruction will pay for it, but he who respects a command will be rewarded.

14 The teaching of the wise is a spring of life, to turn from the snares of death.

15 Good understanding wins favor; but the way of the unfaithful is hard.

16 Every prudent man acts from knowledge, but a fool exposes folly.

17 A wicked messenger falls into trouble, but a trustworthy envoy gains healing.

18 Poverty and shame come to him who refuses discipline, but he who heeds correction shall be honored.

19 Longing fulfilled is sweet to the soul, but fools detest turning from evil.

20 One who walks with wise men grows wise, but a companion of fools suffers harm.

21 Misfortune pursues sinners, but prosperity rewards the righteous.

22 A good man leaves an inheritance to his children's children, but the wealth of the sinner is stored for the righteous.

23 An abundance of food is in poor people's fields, but injustice sweeps it away.

24 One who spares the rod hates his son, but one who loves him is careful to discipline him.

25 The righteous one eats to the satisfying of his soul, but the belly of the wicked goes hungry.

Thoughts to Reflect Upon:

Why is it important to follow the wisdom of godly mentors in our lives? How can you benefit from a relationship with a Christian mentor? How does accountability lead to growth in our faith? Why can we trust God with every aspect of our lives? How does trusting Him lead to prosperity?

Verse of the Day: 13/   Date:

_____
_____
_____

Journal/Notes Section-

_____
_____
_____
_____
_____
_____
_____
_____
_____
_____
_____
_____
_____
_____
_____
_____
_____
_____

Proverbs 14: The Reward of Honest Work

There is a strong warning in this chapter. "The unfaithful will be repaid for his own ways; likewise, a good man will be rewarded for his ways." What are the ways of the unfaithful and foolish man? He is an unreasonable person, lying, despising the truth, refusing to repent, gullible, loose in his speech, and quick to anger and to plot evil. By following the wisdom in Proverbs, we can stay away from the foolish man, seek God in all our ways, and build our own house.

We are to work with our own hands to give generously to the poor. When we make money, we make friends. God is the one who ultimately makes us rich, and He delights in us when we help those in need. We are never to oppress the poor but are to treat everyone equally. A wicked person oppresses others, but by following the path of righteousness, we obtain life.

We must redefine what it means to be rich and poor in this life. When the apostles like Paul worked, they worked to support the ministry Jesus gave them. Their work was an offering to the Lord. It's crucial that we remember this and live it out in our lives.

"For you remember, brothers, our labor and travail; for working night and day, that we might not burden any of you, we preached to you the Good News of God" (1 Thessalonians 2:9).

True wealth is not about accumulating large sums of money. True wealth is about having a vibrant faith, a godly perspective, and doing the work of God's Kingdom. If the storehouses of our soul are filled to the brim with faith in God, then we are rich beyond measure.

That means, instead of striving to achieve worldly wealth—a pursuit that often promotes bad character—we must put our full effort into becoming rich in God's sight.

Proverbs 14: Scripture

Every Wise Woman Builds Her House

1 Every wise woman builds her house, but the foolish one tears it down with her own hands.

2 He who walks in his uprightness fears Yahweh, but he who is perverse in his ways despises him.

3 The fool's talk brings a rod to his back, but the lips of the wise protect them.

4 Where no oxen are, the crib is clean, but much increase is by the strength of the ox.

5 A truthful witness will not lie, but a false witness pours out lies.

6 A scoffer seeks wisdom, and doesn't find it, but knowledge comes easily to a discerning person.

7 Stay away from a foolish man, for you won't find knowledge on his lips.

8 The wisdom of the prudent is to think about his way, but the folly of fools is deceit.

9 Fools mock at making atonement for sins, but among the upright there is good will.

10 The heart knows its own bitterness and joy; he will not share these with a stranger.

11 The house of the wicked will be overthrown, but the tent of the upright will flourish.

12 There is a way which seems right to a man, but in the end it leads to death.

13 Even in laughter the heart may be sorrowful, and mirth may end in heaviness.

14 The unfaithful will be repaid for his own ways; likewise a good man will be rewarded for his ways.

15 A simple man believes everything, but the prudent man carefully considers his ways.

16 A wise man fears, and shuns evil, but the fool is hotheaded and reckless.

17 He who is quick to become angry will commit folly, and a crafty man is hated.

18 The simple inherit folly, but the prudent are crowned with knowledge.

19 The evil bow down before the good, and the wicked at the gates of the righteous.

20 The poor person is shunned even by his own neighbor, but the rich person has many friends.

21 He who despises his neighbor sins, but blessed is he who has pity on the poor.

22 Don't they go astray who plot evil? But love and faithfulness belong to those who plan good.

23 In all hard work there is profit, but the talk of the lips leads only to poverty.

24 The crown of the wise is their riches, but the folly of fools crowns them with folly.

25 A truthful witness saves souls, but a false witness is deceitful.

26 In the fear of Yahweh is a secure fortress, and he will be a refuge for his children.

27 The fear of Yahweh is a fountain of life, turning people from the snares of death.

28 In the multitude of people is the king's glory, but in the lack of people is the destruction of the prince.

29 He who is slow to anger has great understanding, but he who has a quick temper displays folly.

30 The life of the body is a heart at peace, but envy rots the bones.

31 He who oppresses the poor shows contempt for his Maker, but he who is kind to the needy honors him.

32 The wicked is brought down in his calamity, but in death, the righteous has a refuge.

33 Wisdom rests in the heart of one who has understanding, and is even made known in the inward part of fools.

34 Righteousness exalts a nation, but sin is a disgrace to any people.

35 The king's favor is toward a servant who deals wisely, but his wrath is toward one who causes shame.

Thoughts to Reflect Upon:

What does it mean to seek God in all our ways? How does doing so keep us from foolishness? What is the godly vision of true wealth vs. that of the world? Which are you seeking in your life? Why does God wish that we work hard to accumulate true wealth?

Verse of the Day: 14/   Date:

Journal/Notes Section-

Proverbs 15: Words That Speak Life

"Yahweh's eyes are everywhere, keeping watch on the evil and the good." At all times, God is working for those who follow Him as His children and seek righteousness. God does not hide anything from us. Suppose we don't follow God's instruction. In that case, we end up experiencing the discipline we deserve: "There is stern discipline for one who forsakes the way: Whoever hates reproof shall die."

In light of this, it's crucial that we are diligent in rooting out sin in our lives. We can never embrace sin and let it control us. When we do, it's a quick path to ruin. We must continually turn to the Lord and repent so that we can be clothed in the righteousness of Christ.

Again, we must carefully consider what we say to others, for our tongues can bring either healing or destruction. In Western culture, we are taught to speak openly from a young age and express our opinions freely, but wisdom says to count the cost of our words. It is not wise to let our emotions run ahead of us. We must speak the truth in love if we are to build the Kingdom. "The tongue of the wise commends knowledge" and constantly speaks life.

Pray and consider how you use your words. How might the way you speak be affecting others? Do your words build others up, or tear them down?

Commit to only speaking words of life into the hearts of others. Pray that God would strengthen you and teach you how to build others up through the way you speak. In doing so, you will be feeding into the faith of others and honoring the Lord.

Proverbs 15: Scripture

A Gentle Answer Turns away Wrath

1 A gentle answer turns away wrath, but a harsh word stirs up anger.

2 The tongue of the wise commends knowledge, but the mouth of fools gush out folly.

3 Yahweh's eyes are everywhere, keeping watch on the evil and the good.

4 A gentle tongue is a tree of life, but deceit in it crushes the spirit.

5 A fool despises his father's correction, but he who heeds reproof shows prudence.

6 In the house of the righteous is much treasure, but the income of the wicked brings trouble.

7 The lips of the wise spread knowledge; not so with the heart of fools.

8 The sacrifice made by the wicked is an abomination to Yahweh, but the prayer of the upright is his delight.

9 The way of the wicked is an abomination to Yahweh, but he loves him who follows after righteousness.

10 There is stern discipline for one who forsakes the way: whoever hates reproof shall die.

11 Sheol and Abaddon are before Yahweh— how much more then the hearts of the children of men!

12 A scoffer doesn't love to be reproved; he will not go to the wise.

13 A glad heart makes a cheerful face; but an aching heart breaks the spirit.

14 The heart of one who has understanding seeks knowledge, but the mouths of fools feed on folly.

15 All the days of the afflicted are wretched, but one who has a cheerful heart enjoys a continual feast.

16 Better is little, with the fear of Yahweh, than great treasure with trouble.

17 Better is a dinner of herbs, where love is, than a fattened calf with hatred.

18 A wrathful man stirs up contention, but one who is slow to anger appeases strife.

19 The way of the sluggard is like a thorn patch, but the path of the upright is a highway.

20 A wise son makes a father glad, but a foolish man despises his mother.

21 Folly is joy to one who is void of wisdom, but a man of understanding keeps his way straight.

22 Where there is no counsel, plans fail; but in a multitude of counselors they are established.

23 Joy comes to a man with the reply of his mouth. How good is a word at the right time!

24 The path of life leads upward for the wise, to keep him from going downward to Sheol.

25 Yahweh will uproot the house of the proud, but he will keep the widow's borders intact.

26 Yahweh detests the thoughts of the wicked, but the thoughts of the pure are pleasing.

27 He who is greedy for gain troubles his own house, but he who hates bribes will live.

28 The heart of the righteous weighs answers, but the mouth of the wicked gushes out evil.

29 Yahweh is far from the wicked, but he hears the prayer of the righteous.

30 The light of the eyes rejoices the heart. Good news gives health to the bones.

31 The ear that listens to reproof lives, and will be at home among the wise.

32 He who refuses correction despises his own soul, but he who listens to reproof gets understanding.

33 The fear of Yahweh teaches wisdom. Before honor is humility.

Thoughts to Reflect Upon:

How does God's watchful eye influence your actions? Why must we be diligent in rooting out sin in our lives? Why is it important that we be mindful of our words? How does feeding into the lives of others bring honor to the Lord?

Verse of the Day: 15/   Date:

_____
_____
_____

Journal/Notes Section-

_____
_____
_____
_____
_____
_____
_____
_____
_____
_____
_____
_____
_____
_____
_____
_____
_____

Proverbs 16: Ruling One's Spirit

We can make the most elaborate of plans, but God is the one who determines the outcome. There are no kings or politicians who can circumvent the will of God. "Yahweh has made everything for its own end - Yes, even the wicked for the day of evil."

God is well aware of our innermost thoughts and desires, and He judges our intentions. "All the ways of a man are clean in his own eyes; But Yahweh weighs the motives." Is there anything over which you have complete control? Yes, your tongue. I suggest you use it wisely. The words of your mouth are dictated to by your heart, so let us all have control over our emotions if we want to influence others in a positive way. "One who is slow to anger is better than the mighty; one who rules his spirit, than he who takes a city."

We must measure all of our words and actions against the glorious standard that is the Word of God. It's essential that we know God's Word so well that it comes to shape our thoughts, actions, and attitude. If we don't, all of these things will end up being shaped by the ways of the world and not by the ways of God. That will only lead us to living ungodly lives.

Ultimately, no matter what we say or do, God's plans will come to pass. It is foolishness to do anything contrary to God's Will because it will bear no fruit in the world or in our lives! The things of this world are temporary, but the things of God are eternal. That's why we must choose to live by God's ways and seek to fulfill His divine purpose for our lives.

Proverbs 16: Scripture

The Tongue's Answer is from the Lord

1 The plans of the heart belong to man, but the answer of the tongue is from Yahweh.

2 All the ways of a man are clean in his own eyes; but Yahweh weighs the motives.

3 Commit your deeds to Yahweh, and your plans shall succeed.

4 Yahweh has made everything for its own end— yes, even the wicked for the day of evil.

5 Everyone who is proud in heart is an abomination to Yahweh: they shall certainly not be unpunished.

6 By mercy and truth iniquity is atoned for. By the fear of Yahweh men depart from evil.

7 When a man's ways please Yahweh, he makes even his enemies to be at peace with him.

8 Better is a little with righteousness, than great revenues with injustice.

9 A man's heart plans his course, but Yahweh directs his steps.

10 Inspired judgments are on the lips of the king. He shall not betray his mouth.

11 Honest balances and scales are Yahweh's; all the weights in the bag are his work.

12 It is an abomination for kings to do wrong, for the throne is established by righteousness.

13 Righteous lips are the delight of kings. They value one who speaks the truth.

14 The king's wrath is a messenger of death, but a wise man will pacify it.

15 In the light of the king's face is life. His favor is like a cloud of the spring rain.

16 How much better it is to get wisdom than gold! Yes, to get understanding is to be chosen rather than silver.

17 The highway of the upright is to depart from evil. He who keeps his way preserves his soul.

18 Pride goes before destruction, and a haughty spirit before a fall.

19 It is better to be of a lowly spirit with the poor, than to divide the plunder with the proud.

20 He who heeds the Word finds prosperity. Whoever trusts in Yahweh is blessed.

21 The wise in heart shall be called prudent. Pleasantness of the lips promotes instruction.

22 Understanding is a fountain of life to one who has it, but the punishment of fools is their folly.

23 The heart of the wise instructs his mouth, and adds learning to his lips.

24 Pleasant words are a honeycomb, sweet to the soul, and health to the bones.

25 There is a way which seems right to a man, but in the end it leads to death.

26 The appetite of the laboring man labors for him; for his mouth urges him on.

27 A worthless man devises mischief. His speech is like a scorching fire.

28 A perverse man stirs up strife. A whisperer separates close friends.

29 A man of violence entices his neighbor, and leads him in a way that is not good.

30 One who winks his eyes to plot perversities, one who compresses his lips, is bent on evil.

31 Gray hair is a crown of glory. It is attained by a life of righteousness.

32 One who is slow to anger is better than the mighty; one who rules his spirit, than he who takes a city.

33 The lot is cast into the lap, but its every decision is from Yahweh.

Thoughts to Reflect Upon:

Do you truly believe God is in control? How do you feel that He knows your innermost thoughts and desires? How can you best align your heart with Him? How can you best control your tongue? Why is doing the Lord's Will so incredibly important? Is your life aligned with God's plans? If not, how can you get there?

Verse of the Day: 16/   Date:

_____
_____
_____

Journal/Notes Section-

_____
_____
_____
_____
_____
_____
_____
_____
_____
_____
_____
_____
_____
_____
_____
_____
_____
_____
_____

Proverbs 17: Flee from Strife

It is best to steer away from strife at all costs. In life, we should pick our battles and avoid useless arguments. Wherever possible, we should overlook an offense: "He who covers an offense promotes love; But he who repeats a matter separates best friends." It is better to seek forgiveness, let go, and move on than repeat a matter. "The beginning of strife is like breaching a dam," and the harm in repeating an offense is great. But the healing in forgiveness is greater.

Remember, the goal of the Christian life is to become increasingly more like Christ. Jesus forgave endlessly and brought us salvation. We must follow His example and forgive generously as well.

When you forgive, you are denying sin and evil's power over you. You also bring healing to yourself and the person who has offended you when you follow Jesus' example of forgiveness! On the other hand, when you insult the poor, repay righteousness with evil, and praise the wicked, you are dishonoring God.

When you don't know how to speak words of life into a situation, here's an excellent tip: say nothing! "Even a fool, when he keeps silent, is counted wise. When he shuts his lips, he is thought to be discerning."

Remember, you cannot take hurtful words back. Once they are released from your mouth, they have done their damage. It's better to never speak them at all than try to repair the damage they have caused.

Proverbs 17: Scripture

Better a Dry Morsel with Quietness

1 Better is a dry morsel with quietness, than a house full of feasting with strife.

2 A servant who deals wisely will rule over a son who causes shame, and shall have a part in the in heritance among the brothers.

3 The refining pot is for silver, and the furnace for gold, but Yahweh tests the hearts.

4 An evildoer heeds wicked lips. A liar gives ear to a mischievous tongue.

5 Whoever mocks the poor reproaches his Maker. He who is glad at calamity shall not be unpunished.

6 Children's children are the crown of old men; the glory of children are their parents.

7 Arrogant speech isn't fitting for a fool, much less do lying lips fit a prince.

8 A bribe is a precious stone in the eyes of him who gives it; wherever he turns, he prospers.

9 He who covers an offense promotes love; but he who repeats a matter separates best friends.

10 A rebuke enters deeper into one who has understanding than a hundred lashes into a fool.

11 An evil man seeks only rebellion; therefore a cruel messenger shall be sent against him.

12 Let a bear robbed of her cubs meet a man, rather than a fool in his folly.

13 Whoever rewards evil for good, evil shall not depart from his house.

14 The beginning of strife is like breaching a dam, therefore stop contention before quarreling breaks out.

15 He who justifies the wicked, and he who condemns the righteous, both of them alike are an abomination to Yahweh.

16 Why is there money in the hand of a fool to buy wisdom, since he has no understanding?

17 A friend loves at all times; and a brother is born for adversity.

18 A man void of understanding strikes hands, and becomes collateral in the presence of his neighbor.

19 He who loves disobedience loves strife. One who builds a high gate seeks destruction.

20 One who has a perverse heart doesn't find prosperity, and one who has a deceitful tongue falls into trouble.

21 He who becomes the father of a fool grieves. The father of a fool has no joy.

22 A cheerful heart makes good medicine, but a crushed spirit dries up the bones.

23 A wicked man receives a bribe in secret, to pervert the ways of justice.

24 Wisdom is before the face of one who has understanding, but the eyes of a fool wander to the ends of the earth.

25 A foolish son brings grief to his father, and bitterness to her who bore him.

26 Also to punish the righteous is not good, nor to flog officials for their integrity.

27 He who spares his words has knowledge. He who is even tempered is a man of understanding.

28 Even a fool, when he keeps silent, is counted wise. When he shuts his lips, he is thought to be discerning.

Thoughts to Reflect Upon:

Why should we flee from strife at all costs? What does it mean to overlook an offense? How does doing so make us more like Christ? How does forgiveness rob evil of its power? Why should you be silent if you don't have any life-giving words to say?

Verse of the Day: 17/   Date:

_____
_____
_____

Journal/Notes Section-

_____
_____
_____
_____
_____
_____
_____
_____
_____
_____
_____
_____
_____
_____
_____
_____
_____
_____

Proverbs 18: Death and Life in the Tongue

We all have the "friend" who isolates himself, the one who withdraws from people to pursue his selfish ways. "An unfriendly man pursues selfishness, and defies all sound judgment." We are stronger together, and God wants us to be connected as partners or coworkers.

God's very design for us is to thrive in all relationships. That's why we have a natural desire to pursue them. But sometimes, that desire gets buried under all the pressures of the world and we draw inward toward self-centeredness. We must avoid this tendency at all costs. No matter what life may bring, it's essential that we focus on the relationships God has put in our lives.

Solomon repeatedly mentions that we are not to favor the guilty, even if they are our close associates or friends. To do so is wickedness, which leads to disgrace. God is ultimately our protector against those who favor the guilty. On the other hand, it is a blessing to have a faithful friend. A "man of many companions may be ruined, but there is a friend who sticks closer than a brother," and there's no friend more faithful than Jesus! Let us cling to Him in everything!

In our restless society, we tend to shoot off our mouths without giving it much thought. But know that "A fool's lips come into strife, And his mouth invites beatings." How many arguments have you seen on social media? Just click on the comments section of any popular social media post, and you will see hurtful, senseless arguing. This is precisely the kind of fruitless arguments which we must avoid. They do nothing but perpetuate the sinful nature within our hearts.

Proverbs 18: Scripture

The Unfriendly Pursue Selfishness

1 An unfriendly man pursues selfishness, and defies all sound judgment.

2 A fool has no delight in understanding, but only in revealing his own opinion.

3 When wickedness comes, contempt also comes, and with shame comes disgrace.

4 The words of a man's mouth are like deep waters. The fountain of wisdom is like a flowing brook.

5 To be partial to the faces of the wicked is not good, nor to deprive the innocent of justice.

6 A fool's lips come into strife, and his mouth invites beatings.

7 A fool's mouth is his destruction, and his lips are a snare to his soul.

8 The words of a gossip are like dainty morsels: they go down into a person's innermost parts.

9 One who is slack in his work is brother to him who is a master of destruction.

10 The name of Yahweh is a strong tower: the righteous run to him, and are safe.

11 The rich man's wealth is his strong city, like an unscalable wall in his own imagination.

12 Before destruction the heart of man is proud, but before honor is humility.

13 He who gives answer before he hears, that is folly and shame to him.

14 A man's spirit will sustain him in sickness, but a crushed spirit, who can bear?

15 The heart of the discerning gets knowledge. The ear of the wise seeks knowledge.

16 A man's gift makes room for him, and brings him before great men.

17 He who pleads his cause first seems right; until another comes and questions him.

18 The lot settles disputes, and keeps strong ones apart.

19 A brother offended is more difficult than a fortified city; and disputes are like the bars of a castle.

20 A man's stomach is filled with the fruit of his mouth. With the harvest of his lips he is satisfied.

21 Death and life are in the power of the tongue; those who love it will eat its fruit.

22 Whoever finds a wife finds a good thing, and obtains favor of Yahweh.

23 The poor plead for mercy, but the rich answer harshly.

24 A man of many companions may be ruined, but there is a friend who sticks closer than a brother.

Thoughts to Reflect Upon:

Why are the relationships God has given us so important? How can we honor them in this life? How does living out healthy relationships please God? In business transactions, how can we still honor our relationships and avoid selfishness?

Verse of the Day: 18/   Date:

Journal/Notes Section-

Proverbs 19: God's Counsel Prevails

As you read through Chapter 19, you will realize much of the same advice is repeated. This only reinforces its value. Anything in life that's worth doing takes repetition in order to bear fruit in our lives. The same is true of God's Word!

"Better is the poor who walks in his integrity than he who is perverse in his lips and is a fool." God doesn't want us to be obsessed with money or use dishonest means to obtain riches. It is better to have integrity than to be rich. "Wealth adds many friends, But the poor is separated from his friend," though Solomon does not say if wealth brings *true* friends. Many people avoid the poor; however, God wants us to visit them and minister to them. "He who has pity on the poor lends to Yahweh; He will reward him."

Speaking from personal experience, I and many others have had a lot of enthusiastic ideas for attaining fame and fortune, but now some have changed. "There are many plans in a man's heart, But Yahweh's counsel will prevail." We can plan, but ultimately God's way will prevail. Eventually, the Book of Revelation will play out, regardless.

That means in the present, we must live according to God's ways. His Word will bear fruit in our lives, making us rich in every way, and preparing us for the times that are to come. And don't dread those times, as some are in the habit of doing! When they come, we will meet our loving Creator face to face and begin our eternity in His everlasting Kingdom. There, peace, harmony, and love will reign forever.

Proverbs 19: Scripture

Better is the Poor Man with Integrity

1 Better is the poor who walks in his integrity than he who is perverse in his lips and is a fool.

2 It isn't good to have zeal without knowledge; nor being hasty with one's feet and missing the way.

3 The foolishness of man subverts his way; his heart rages against Yahweh.

4 Wealth adds many friends, but the poor is separated from his friend.

5 A false witness shall not be unpunished. He who pours out lies shall not go free.

6 Many will entreat the favor of a ruler, and everyone is a friend to a man who gives gifts.

7 All the relatives of the poor shun him: how much more do his friends avoid him! He pursues them with pleas, but they are gone.

8 He who gets wisdom loves his own soul. He who keeps understanding shall find good.

9 A false witness shall not be unpunished. He who utters lies shall perish.

10 Delicate living is not appropriate for a fool, much less for a servant to have rule over princes.

11 The discretion of a man makes him slow to anger. It is his glory to overlook an offense.

12 The king's wrath is like the roaring of a lion, but his favor is like dew on the grass.

13 A foolish son is the calamity of his father. A wife's quarrels are a continual dripping.

14 House and riches are an inheritance from fathers, but a prudent wife is from Yahweh.

15 Slothfulness casts into a deep sleep. The idle soul shall suffer hunger.

16 He who keeps the commandment keeps his soul, but he who is contemptuous in his ways shall die.

17 He who has pity on the poor lends to Yahweh; he will reward him.

18 Discipline your son, for there is hope; don't be a willing party to his death.

19 A hot-tempered man must pay the penalty, for if you rescue him, you must do it again.

20 Listen to counsel and receive instruction, that you may be wise in your latter end.

21 There are many plans in a man's heart, but Yahweh's counsel will prevail.

22 That which makes a man to be desired is his kindness. A poor man is better than a liar.

23 The fear of Yahweh leads to life, then contentment; he rests and will not be touched by trouble.

24 The sluggard buries his hand in the dish; he will not so much as bring it to his mouth again.

25 Flog a scoffer, and the simple will learn prudence; rebuke one who has understanding, and he will gain knowledge.

26 He who robs his father and drives away his mother, is a son who causes shame and brings reproach.

27 If you stop listening to instruction, my son, you will stray from the words of knowledge.

28 A corrupt witness mocks justice, and the mouth of the wicked gulps down iniquity.

29 Penalties are prepared for scoffers, and beatings for the backs of fools.

Thoughts to Reflect Upon:

Why is it foolishness to live for our own desires? Why is the pursuit of wealth and fame fruitless, and what should be our motivations in life instead? How can we best use our resources instead of hoarding them for ourselves? How can we live according to God's ways in the present?

Verse of the Day: 19/   Date:

_____
_____
_____

Journal/Notes Section-

_____
_____
_____
_____
_____
_____
_____
_____
_____
_____
_____
_____
_____
_____
_____
_____
_____
_____

Proverbs 20: Mind Your Company

We all have seen the drunk—they are foolhardy and easily led astray. God warns us by opening with: "Wine is a mocker, strong drink a brawler, and whoever is led astray by it is not wise." We can almost expect this from the world. Nonetheless, often enough, we see Christians who know the Lord yet suffer from such foolishness.

As believers, we must hold ourselves to a different standard than the world's. God has called us to be witnesses of the Gospel and shining lights in a world full of darkness. If we mingle with that darkness, we will not be the witnesses we are called to be. Instead, we will simply blend in with the crowd.

The Lord's countless warnings about being lazy make it clear that He does not want us to be idle. We must work diligently toward the calling God has put upon our lives. There is much to be done for God's Kingdom, and He has given each of us a special role to play in His plan.

We are also to be wise in our choice of companions: "Therefore do not associate with a simple babbler … He who goes about as a tale-bearer reveals secrets; Therefore don't keep company with him who opens wide his lips." To be true witnesses to the Gospel and live out the purpose He has given us, we must walk through life with like-minded believers. They will encourage us on our path and give us that extra motivation to live out our purpose.

Lastly, we are never to take vengeance on our own. Do not repay the evildoer with evil, for vengeance belongs to God. We can trust that God will repay the wicked at the right time, for He is the ultimate judge. It is not something to take into our own hands.

Proverbs 20: Scripture

Wine is a Mocker

1 Wine is a mocker, and beer is a brawler. Whoever is led astray by them is not wise.

2 The terror of a king is like the roaring of a lion. He who provokes him to anger forfeits his own life.

3 It is an honor for a man to keep aloof from strife; but every fool will be quarreling.

4 The sluggard will not plow by reason of the winter; therefore he shall beg in harvest, and have nothing.

5 Counsel in the heart of man is like deep water; but a man of understanding will draw it out.

6 Many men claim to be men of unfailing love, but who can find a faithful man?

7 A righteous man walks in integrity. Blessed are his children after him.

8 A king who sits on the throne of judgment scatters away all evil with his eyes.

9 Who can say, "I have made my heart pure. I am clean and without sin?"

10 Differing weights and differing measures, both of them alike are an abomination to Yahweh.

11 Even a child makes himself known by his doings, whether his work is pure, and whether it is right.

12 The hearing ear, and the seeing eye, Yahweh has made even both of them.

13 Don't love sleep, lest you come to poverty. Open your eyes, and you shall be satisfied with bread.

14 "It's no good, it's no good," says the buyer; but when he is gone his way, then he boasts.

15 There is gold and abundance of rubies; but the lips of knowledge are a rare jewel.

16 Take the garment of one who puts up collateral for a stranger; and hold him in pledge for a wayward woman.

17 Fraudulent food is sweet to a man, but afterwards his mouth is filled with gravel.

18 Plans are established by advice; by wise guidance you wage war!

19 He who goes about as a tale-bearer reveals secrets; therefore don't keep company with him who opens wide his lips.

20 Whoever curses his father or his mother, his lamp shall be put out in blackness of darkness.

21 An inheritance quickly gained at the beginning, won't be blessed in the end.

22 Don't say, "I will pay back evil." Wait for Yahweh, and he will save you.

23 Yahweh detests differing weights, and dishonest scales are not pleasing.

24 A man's steps are from Yahweh; how then can man understand his way?

25 It is a snare to a man to make a rash dedication, then later to consider his vows.

26 A wise king winnows out the wicked, and drives the threshing wheel over them.

27 The spirit of man is Yahweh's lamp, searching all his innermost parts.

28 Love and faithfulness keep the king safe. His throne is sustained by love.

29 The glory of young men is their strength. The splendor of old men is their gray hair.

30 Wounding blows cleanse away evil, and beatings purge the innermost parts.

Thoughts to Reflect Upon:

Why is it important that we stay away from drunkenness? What kind of dangers does that lead us into? Why does God hold us to different standards than the people of the world do? How can we live as witnesses to Christ? Why is laziness a destructive thing? Why should we flee from wanting to take vengeance?

Verse of the Day: 20/   Date:

_____
_____
_____

Journal/Notes Section-

_____
_____
_____
_____
_____
_____
_____
_____
_____
_____
_____
_____
_____
_____
_____
_____

Proverbs 21: Why Pray for Your Leaders?

We are instructed to, first and foremost, pray for kings (our government) and those in authority. We are to pray for them so they will do good and follow the will of the Lord (1 Timothy 2:2). "The king's heart is in Yahweh's hand like the watercourses. He turns it wherever he desires."

We are never to "judge" another person's heart, for only God judges righteously. "Every way of a man is right in his own eyes, But Yahweh weighs the hearts." This includes the hearts of our leaders. While we don't have to agree with every decision they make, it's important that we pray for them and leave the judgment of them to the Lord. Even if they are doing things contrary to the Lord's will, they will experience the consequences of their actions in due time. But that will happen at God's hand, not ours.

Again, "To do righteousness and justice is more acceptable to Yahweh than sacrifice." No amount of good works—whether in church or elsewhere—means anything if we do not obey God's instructions. We should not be everything to everyone but rather be the person God wants us to be according to His specific purpose in our lives. When we allow Him to mold and shape us through His Holy Spirit inside of us, we will live out the fullness of our potential in Christ.

Again, God warns us about being careful in our associations to protect us against future pain. Never forget that keeping bad company will only serve to hold you back from the incredible things God has called you to do. Not only that, but it will also compromise your character. Minister to those in need, no matter where they are on their journey, but let your close friends only be like-minded believers in the Lord.

Proverbs 21: Scripture

The King's Heart is in the Lord's Hand

1 The king's heart is in Yahweh's hand like the watercourses. He turns it wherever he desires.

2 Every way of a man is right in his own eyes, but Yahweh weighs the hearts.

3 To do righteousness and justice is more acceptable to Yahweh than sacrifice.

4 A high look, and a proud heart, the lamp of the wicked, is sin.

5 The plans of the diligent surely lead to profit; and everyone who is hasty surely rushes to poverty.

6 Getting treasures by a lying tongue is a fleeting vapor for those who seek death.

7 The violence of the wicked will drive them away, because they refuse to do what is right.

8 The way of the guilty is devious, but the conduct of the innocent is upright.

9 It is better to dwell in the corner of the housetop, than to share a house with a contentious woman.

10 The soul of the wicked desires evil; his neighbor finds no mercy in his eyes.

11 When the mocker is punished, the simple gains wisdom. When the wise is instructed, he receives knowledge.

12 The Righteous One considers the house of the wicked, and brings the wicked to ruin.

13 Whoever stops his ears at the cry of the poor, he will also cry out, but shall not be heard.

14 A gift in secret pacifies anger; and a bribe in the cloak, strong wrath.

15 It is joy to the righteous to do justice; but it is a destruction to the workers of iniquity.

16 The man who wanders out of the way of understanding shall rest in the assembly of the dead.

17 He who loves pleasure shall be a poor man. He who loves wine and oil shall not be rich.

18 The wicked is a ransom for the righteous; the treacherous for the upright.

19 It is better to dwell in a desert land, than with a contentious and fretful woman.

20 There is precious treasure and oil in the dwelling of the wise; but a foolish man swallows it up.

21 He who follows after righteousness and kindness finds life, righteousness, and honor.

22 A wise man scales the city of the mighty, and brings down the strength of its confidence.

23 Whoever guards his mouth and his tongue keeps his soul from troubles.

24 The proud and haughty man, "scoffer" is his name; he works in the arrogance of pride.

25 The desire of the sluggard kills him, for his hands refuse to labor.

26 There are those who covet greedily all day long; but the righteous give and don't withhold.

27 The sacrifice of the wicked is an abomination: how much more, when he brings it with a wicked mind!

28 A false witness will perish, and a man who listens speaks to eternity.

29 A wicked man hardens his face; but as for the upright, he establishes his ways.

30 There is no wisdom nor understanding nor counsel against Yahweh.

31 The horse is prepared for the day of battle; but victory is with Yahweh.

Thoughts to Reflect Upon:

Why is it important to pray for our leaders? Why should God alone be the one to judge the hearts of others? Why is living righteously more important than any kind of sacrifice? How does keeping healthy associations protect us from future pain?

Verse of the Day: 21/   Date:

_____
_____
_____

Journal/Notes Section-

_____
_____
_____
_____
_____
_____
_____
_____
_____
_____
_____
_____
_____
_____
_____
_____
_____
_____
_____
_____

Proverbs 22: A Good Name

"A good name is more desirable than great riches; Loving favor rather than silver and gold." Since reputation is more valuable than wealth, it is not wise to pursue riches at the expense of your integrity. Those who borrow will end up being a servant to the lender. The world is facing a debt crisis, and the Bible warns about the consequences of mounting debt, for we will be at the mercy of the bankers and global elite.

God warns us so strongly in this area because He desires that we would experience true freedom in every way: freedom from sin, and, yes, financial freedom! He wants us to be able to be in a position to give back to our local church and help fuel the ministries that are making a difference in the world for His everlasting Kingdom.

"Train up a child in the way he should go, And when he is old he will not depart from it." There are many blessings a parent or elder can bestow on a child. A pastor can offer recognition and leadership, but it can be empty without the guidance of a mentor. The most important thing we can do is teach someone the way so that they will hold on to their faith when they are pressured by worldly things when they are older.

A solid foundation of faith will serve someone throughout their entire lives. The earlier they can build that foundation in their lives, the better. That gives them time to develop a vibrant and life-giving worldview which will enrich every aspect of their lives.

Proverbs 22: Scripture

A Good Name More Desirable Than Riches

1 A good name is more desirable than great riches, and loving favor is better than silver and gold.

2 The rich and the poor have this in common: Yahweh is the maker of them all.

3 A prudent man sees danger, and hides himself; but the simple pass on, and suffer for it.

4 The result of humility and the fear of Yahweh is wealth, honor, and life.

5 Thorns and snares are in the path of the wicked: whoever guards his soul stays from them.

6 Train up a child in the way he should go, and when he is old he will not depart from it.

7 The rich rule over the poor. The borrower is servant to the lender.

8 He who sows wickedness reaps trouble, and the rod of his fury will be destroyed.

9 He who has a generous eye will be blessed; for he shares his food with the poor.

10 Drive out the mocker, and strife will go out; yes, quarrels and insults will stop.

11 He who loves purity of heart and speaks gracefully is the king's friend.

12 The eyes of Yahweh watch over knowledge; but he frustrates the words of the unfaithful.

13 The sluggard says, "There is a lion outside! I will be killed in the streets!"

14 The mouth of an adulteress is a deep pit: he who is under Yahweh's wrath will fall into it.

15 Folly is bound up in the heart of a child: the rod of discipline drives it far from him.

16 Whoever oppresses the poor for his own increase and whoever gives to the rich, both come to poverty.

17 Turn your ear, and listen to the words of the wise. Apply your heart to my teaching.

18 For it is a pleasant thing if you keep them within you, if all of them are ready on your lips.

19 That your trust may be in Yahweh, I teach you today, even you.

20 Haven't I written to you thirty excellent things of counsel and knowledge,

21 To teach you truth, reliable words, to give sound answers to the ones who sent you?

22 Don't exploit the poor, because he is poor; and don't crush the needy in court;

23 for Yahweh will plead their case, and plunder the life of those who plunder them.

24 Don't befriend a hot-tempered man, and don't associate with one who harbors anger:

25 lest you learn his ways, and ensnare your soul.

26 Don't you be one of those who strike hands, of those who are collateral for debts.

27 If you don't have means to pay, why should he take away your bed from under you?

28 Don't move the ancient boundary stone, which your fathers have set up.

29 Do you see a man skilled in his work? He will serve kings. He won't serve obscure men.

Thoughts to Reflect Upon:

Why is reputation more important than wealth? Why does God wish that we're careful with our finances? How does God provide us with freedom in every way? Why is it important that our foundation is firmly in Christ? How will that affect the rest of our lives?

Verse of the Day: 22/   Date:

Journal/Notes Section-

Proverbs 23: Beware of Covetousness

We need to control our appetite, especially in front of a king or someone with power. "Don't be desirous of his dainties, since they are deceitful food." What is behind that pleasant talk and those delicacies are things that may bait you and pull you into evil. If we desire the things the wealthy can afford, they will quickly dissipate.

Interestingly, the richest man of the time, and perhaps in history, warns us about overworking for wealth and its deceitfulness. "Don't weary yourself to be rich. In your wisdom, show restraint." We are to work hard and show godly character in our daily lives, but never to overwork for the deceitfulness of gain. When we overwork, we tend to neglect our relationship with God, family, and people in general. God corrects us more often than we care to admit our faults.

We see the consistent theme of correcting a child and not being a permissive parent. "Punish him with the rod, And save his soul from Sheol." If we love our children, we will ensure they learn godly wisdom and make the right choices based on sound moral values.

We are never to be envious of the bounty of those who reject God and are comfortable with their sin. They may have more money, less stress, or live a better life, but they have no guarantee of a future or eternity. But for those who fear the Lord, "Indeed, surely there is a future hope, and your hope will not be cut off. Listen, my son, and be wise, and keep your heart on the right path." God will always guide our steps if we follow His way. People who live apart from God have no such assurance.

Proverbs 23: Scripture

Diligently Consider What is before You

1 When you sit to eat with a ruler, consider diligently what is before you;

2 put a knife to your throat, if you are a man given to appetite.

3 Don't be desirous of his dainties, since they are deceitful food.

4 Don't weary yourself to be rich. In your wisdom, show restraint.

5 Why do you set your eyes on that which is not? For it certainly sprouts wings like an eagle and flies in the sky.

6 Don't eat the food of him who has a stingy eye, and don't crave his delicacies:

7 for as he thinks about the cost, so he is. "Eat and drink!" he says to you, but his heart is not with you.

8 The morsel which you have eaten you shall vomit up, and lose your good words.

9 Don't speak in the ears of a fool, for he will despise the wisdom of your words.

10 Don't move the ancient boundary stone. Don't encroach on the fields of the fatherless:

11 for their Defender is strong. He will plead their case against you.

12 Apply your heart to instruction, and your ears to the words of knowledge.

13 Don't withhold correction from a child. If you punish him with the rod, he will not die.

14 Punish him with the rod, and save his soul from Sheol.

15 My son, if your heart is wise, then my heart will be glad, even mine:

16 yes, my heart will rejoice, when your lips speak what is right.

17 Don't let your heart envy sinners; but rather fear Yahweh all the day long.

18 Indeed surely there is a future hope, and your hope will not be cut off.

19 Listen, my son, and be wise, and keep your heart on the right path!

20 Don't be among ones drinking too much wine, or those who gorge themselves on meat:

21 for the drunkard and the glutton shall become poor; and drowsiness clothes them in rags.

22 Listen to your father who gave you life, and don't despise your mother when she is old.

23 Buy the truth, and don't sell it. Get wisdom, discipline, and understanding.

24 The father of the righteous has great joy. Whoever fathers a wise child delights in him.

25 Let your father and your mother be glad! Let her who bore you rejoice!

26 My son, give me your heart; and let your eyes keep in my ways.

27 For a prostitute is a deep pit; and a wayward wife is a narrow well.

28 Yes, she lies in wait like a robber, and increases the unfaithful among men.

29 Who has woe? Who has sorrow? Who has strife? Who has complaints? Who has needless bruises? Who has bloodshot eyes?

30 Those who stay long at the wine; those who go to seek out mixed wine.

31 Don't look at the wine when it is red, when it sparkles in the cup, when it goes down smoothly.

32 In the end, it bites like a snake, and poisons like a viper.

33 Your eyes will see strange things, and your mind will imagine confusing things.

34 Yes, you will be as he who lies down in the midst of the sea, or as he who lies on top of the rigging:

35 "They hit me, and I was not hurt! They beat me, and I don't feel it! When will I wake up? I can do it again. I can find another."

Thoughts to Reflect Upon:

Why should we not covet the wealth of others? Why should we not overwork to gain wealth? What are the potential pitfalls of doing so, and why are those risks not worth the reward? Why is it important to lovingly discipline our children? How does it help them to grow up wise?

Verse of the Day: 23/   Date:

_____
_____
_____

Journal/Notes Section-

_____
_____
_____
_____
_____
_____
_____
_____
_____
_____
_____
_____
_____
_____
_____
_____
_____
_____

Proverbs 24: Do Not Envy the Wicked

God is concerned with our innermost desires as revealed by our hearts. If we are obsessed with the things of the world, we move our focus away from kingdom principles. "Don't you be envious against evil men; neither desire to be with them: For their hearts plot violence, and their lips talk about mischief." The character of an evil man is his undoing, whereas a righteous man will fall many times and get back up. Even though the wicked may appear to be better off, they are far from Christ; being self-seeking, they will come to ruin.

We have to find that fine balance of being in the world but not of the world. Our true citizenship and eternal destiny are found in God's everlasting Kingdom. Heaven is our home, not the earth, for we are children of God. When we fully embrace that truth, we will be able to keep our eyes on the things of God and not the things of the world.

That means as we go about this life, we will be focused on doing things that will shape our eternal home and not our current one. We won't be worried about building up wealth and security in this life. Rather, we will be eager to do the things that will reap an eternal reward. We will be able to rest easy, knowing that true wealth and security are found in God's promises and not in the riches of this world.

The sin of commission is when we commit sin with our actions, such as fornication, violence, slander, or similar things. The sin of omission is when we neglect to do what is right. We have the responsibility to "Rescue those who are being led away to death! Indeed, hold back those who are staggering to the slaughter!" Society may say that everybody has the freedom to make their own choice, but if you can save them from death, which option would you choose?

Proverbs 24: Scripture

Don't be Envious of Evil Men

1 Don't be envious of evil men; neither desire to be with them:

2 for their hearts plot violence, and their lips talk about mischief.

3 Through wisdom a house is built; by understanding it is established;

4 by knowledge the rooms are filled with all rare and beautiful treasure.

5 A wise man has great power; and a knowledgeable man increases strength;

6 for by wise guidance you wage your war; and victory is in many advisors.

7 Wisdom is too high for a fool: he doesn't open his mouth in the gate.

8 One who plots to do evil will be called a schemer.

9 The schemes of folly are sin. The mocker is detested by men.

10 If you falter in the time of trouble, your strength is small.

11 Rescue those who are being led away to death! Indeed, hold back those who are staggering to the slaughter!

12 If you say, "Behold, we didn't know this;" doesn't he who weighs the hearts consider it? He who keeps your soul, doesn't he know it? Shall he not render to every man according to his work?

13 My son, eat honey, for it is good; the droppings of the honeycomb, which are sweet to your taste:

14 so you shall know wisdom to be to your soul; if you have found it, then there will be a reward, your hope will not be cut off.

15 Don't lay in wait, wicked man, against the habitation of the righteous. Don't destroy his resting place:

16 for a righteous man falls seven times, and rises up again; but the wicked are overthrown by calamity.

17 Don't rejoice when your enemy falls. Don't let your heart be glad when he is overthrown;

18 lest Yahweh see it, and it displease him, and he turn away his wrath from him.

19 Don't fret yourself because of evildoers; neither be envious of the wicked:

20 for there will be no reward to the evil man; and the lamp of the wicked shall be snuffed out.

21 My son, fear Yahweh and the king. Don't join those who are rebellious:

22 for their calamity will rise suddenly; the destruction from them both—who knows?

Further Sayings of the Wise

23 These also are sayings of the wise. To show partiality in judgment is not good.

24 He who says to the wicked, "You are righteous;" peoples shall curse him, and nations shall abhor him—

25 but it will go well with those who convict the guilty, and a rich blessing will come on them.

26 An honest answer is like a kiss on the lips.

27 Prepare your work outside, and get your fields ready. Afterwards, build your house.

28 Don't be a witness against your neighbor without cause. Don't deceive with your lips.

29 Don't say, "I will do to him as he has done to me; I will render to the man according to his work."

30 I went by the field of the sluggard, by the vineyard of the man void of understanding;

31 Behold, it was all grown over with thorns. Its surface was covered with nettles, and its stone wall was broken down.

32 Then I saw, and considered well. I saw, and received instruction:

33 a little sleep, a little slumber, a little folding of the hands to sleep;

34 so your poverty will come as a robber, and your want as an armed man.

Thoughts to Reflect Upon:

Why is God most concerned with our innermost desires? How can we align such desires with His plan for us? How do we find the balance of living in the world but not being of it? What is the sin of commission? What is the sin of omission? How are these definitions helpful?

Verse of the Day: 24/   Date:

_____
_____
_____

Journal/Notes Section-

_____
_____
_____
_____
_____
_____
_____
_____
_____
_____
_____
_____
_____
_____
_____
_____
_____
_____
_____
_____

Proverbs 25: Set Clear Boundaries

God wants us to respect the privacy of others and establish healthy boundaries. "Let your foot be seldom in your neighbor's house, lest he be weary of you, and hate you." By spending too much time with a friend, church family, or at the "pastor's house," we can cause tension. People need space, and we should not intrude into others' lives or marriages for our own selfish needs.

Establishing and maintaining healthy boundaries is essential for healthy relationships. It does not mean you are not being a hospitable person or loving people the way you should. It just means that you are protecting your relationships and making adequate time for everyone, including yourself!

God is also concerned about whom we marry and with whom we spend our lives serving Him. God says, "It is better to dwell in the corner of the housetop, Than to share a house with a contentious woman." When selecting a partner in marriage, we must find someone who is equally yoked, full of love for God, and not quarrelsome. If not, we will be sure to experience conflict in our marriage.

"Like a city that is broken down and without walls is a man whose spirit is without restraint." Believers are never to overeat, engage in backbiting, give vent to our anger, or seek our own glory. We are required to have the self-control to govern our lives wisely and not give in to temptation.

Self-control will help us to overcome the advances of sin upon our hearts. Temptation is a real adversary, and we must be relentless in fighting against it. If not, sin will surely overtake us, as it is a relentless foe.

Proverbs 25: Scripture

More Proverbs of Solomon

1 These also are proverbs of Solomon, which the men of Hezekiah king of Judah copied out.

2 It is the glory of God to conceal a thing, but the glory of kings is to search out a matter.

3 As the heavens for height, and the earth for depth, so the hearts of kings are unsearchable.

4 Take away the dross from the silver, and material comes out for the refiner;

5 Take away the wicked from the king's presence, and his throne will be established in righteousness.

6 Don't exalt yourself in the presence of the king, or claim a place among great men;

7 for it is better that it be said to you, "Come up here," than that you should be put lower in the presence of the prince, whom your eyes have seen.

8 Don't be hasty in bringing charges to court. What will you do in the end when your neighbor shames you?

9 Debate your case with your neighbor, and don't betray the confidence of another;

10 lest one who hears it put you to shame, and your bad reputation never depart.

11 A word fitly spoken is like apples of gold in settings of silver.

12 As an earring of gold, and an ornament of fine gold, so is a wise reprover to an obedient ear.

13 As the cold of snow in the time of harvest, so is a faithful messenger to those who send him; for he refreshes the soul of his masters.

14 As clouds and wind without rain, so is he who boasts of gifts deceptively.

15 By patience a ruler is persuaded. A soft tongue breaks the bone.

16 Have you found honey? Eat as much as is sufficient for you, lest you eat too much, and vomit it.

17 Let your foot be seldom in your neighbor's house, lest he be weary of you, and hate you.

18 A man who gives false testimony against his neighbor is like a club, a sword, or a sharp arrow.

19 Confidence in someone unfaithful in time of trouble is like a bad tooth, or a lame foot.

20 As one who takes away a garment in cold weather, or vinegar on soda, so is one who sings songs to a heavy heart.

21 If your enemy is hungry, give him food to eat. If he is thirsty, give him water to drink:

22 for you will heap coals of fire on his head, and Yahweh will reward you.

23 The north wind brings forth rain: so a backbiting tongue brings an angry face.

24 It is better to dwell in the corner of the housetop, than to share a house with a contentious woman.

25 Like cold water to a thirsty soul, so is good news from a far country.

26 Like a muddied spring, and a polluted well, so is a righteous man who gives way before the wicked.

27 It is not good to eat much honey; nor is it honorable to seek one's own honor.

28 Like a city that is broken down and without walls is a man whose spirit is without restraint.

Thoughts to Reflect Upon:

Why are healthy boundaries important in every relationship? Why is God concerned with who we marry and spend our time with? How do these choices affect our lives? How does self-control protect us against sin and temptation? How can you develop self-control in your life?

Verse of the Day: 25/   Date:

_____
_____
_____

Journal/Notes Section-

_____
_____
_____
_____
_____
_____
_____
_____
_____
_____
_____
_____
_____
_____
_____
_____
_____

Proverbs 26: The Fool, the Sluggard, and the Gossip

This chapter deals with three sorts of people: the fool, the sluggard, and the gossip.

There is a warning for us not to be a fool, and here are the signs of one. The fool is undeserving of honor, and should he receive it, it is "like snow in summer," totally misplaced. A fool is not to be trusted with a message, nor can he appreciate a wise saying. If you hire him, he will only cause disruption in the workplace. He cannot be corrected: "As a dog that returns to his vomit, So is a fool who repeats his folly."

Then we have the sluggard, who is too lazy to even get out of bed and makes every excuse not to venture out into the street. However, in his own eyes, he is wiser than most. His own distorted perceptions of the world have blinded him to reality.

The gossip is charming, but his heart is full of malice and evil intentions. Take care if you eat with him because of the loose talk that defiles your spirit: "The words of a whisperer are as dainty morsels, they go down into the innermost parts."

We must evaluate our lives and ensure that we do not fall into any of these three categories. It is a good practice to have a consistent time that you evaluate your life against the measuring rod—that is, the Holy Bible.

Come to this practice from a place of prayer, inviting God to show you where you can make improvements and also where you are doing well. While this can be hard, always be open, honest, and vulnerable in this practice. Only then will you experience true growth.

Proverbs 26: Scripture

Similitudes and Instructions

1 Like snow in summer, and as rain in harvest, so honor is not fitting for a fool.

2 Like a fluttering sparrow, like a darting swallow, so the undeserved curse doesn't come to rest.

3 A whip is for the horse, a bridle for the donkey, and a rod for the back of fools!

4 Don't answer a fool according to his folly, lest you also be like him.

5 Answer a fool according to his folly, lest he be wise in his own eyes.

6 One who sends a message by the hand of a fool is cutting off feet and drinking violence.

7 Like the legs of the lame that hang loose: so is a parable in the mouth of fools.

8 As one who binds a stone in a sling, so is he who gives honor to a fool.

9 Like a thornbush that goes into the hand of a drunkard, so is a parable in the mouth of fools.

10 As an archer who wounds all, so is he who hires a fool or he who hires those who pass by.

11 As a dog that returns to his vomit, so is a fool who repeats his folly.

12 Do you see a man wise in his own eyes? There is more hope for a fool than for him.

13 The sluggard says, "There is a lion in the road! A fierce lion roams the streets!"

14 As the door turns on its hinges, so does the sluggard on his bed.

15 The sluggard buries his hand in the dish. He is too lazy to bring it back to his mouth.

16 The sluggard is wiser in his own eyes than seven men who answer with discretion.

17 Like one who grabs a dog's ears is one who passes by and meddles in a quarrel not his own.

18 Like a madman who shoots torches, arrows, and death,

19 is the man who deceives his neighbor and says, "Am I not joking?"

20 For lack of wood a fire goes out. Without gossip, a quarrel dies down.

21 As coals are to hot embers, and wood to fire, so is a contentious man to kindling strife.

22 The words of a whisperer are as dainty morsels, they go down into the innermost parts.

23 Like silver dross on an earthen vessel are the lips of a fervent one with an evil heart.

24 A malicious man disguises himself with his lips, but he harbors evil in his heart.

25 When his speech is charming, don't believe him; for there are seven abominations in his heart.

26 His malice may be concealed by deception, but his wickedness will be exposed in the assembly.

27 Whoever digs a pit shall fall into it. Whoever rolls a stone, it will come back on him.

28 A lying tongue hates those it hurts; and a flattering mouth works ruin.

Thoughts to Reflect Upon:

Who are the fool, the sluggard, and the gossip? Why should we avoid being like them at all costs? Why should we regularly evaluate our lives? What should be the standard we measure them against? How does being open and vulnerable help us in that process?

Verse of the Day: 26/   Date:

Journal/Notes Section-

Proverbs 27: Guard Your Assets

Avoid boasting about yourself or your plans, for only God knows the future. When you begin to trust too much in the plans you have made, you become arrogant and prideful. You end up relying too much on your own ability and forgetting your dependence on God. Make your plans with the Lord, ultimately being ready to surrender your plans to His perfect and glorious Will.

Do not praise yourself: "Let another man praise you, and not your own mouth; A stranger, and not your own lips." Praise from our enemies is suspect because they have hidden motives, but chastisement from a friend is good because it helps us become more Christ-like. There is mutual gain when people of equal caliber collaborate. They can challenge and refine each other: "Iron sharpens iron; so a man sharpens his friend's countenance."

Fellowship is an essential discipline of the Christian life. Through it, God pushes us ever forward to the work He has prepared for us to accomplish. We just must be careful in choosing the right company. We only have so much time, so it's vital to give it to the people who are going to feed into your life and not steal from it.

It is wise to plan your projects ahead, for blessings can come and go. But when you have attended to all that needs to be done, you will reap the fruit of all your hard-earned labor in the right season. When you make your plans by the guidance and direction of the Lord, you can rest assured that they are aligned with His Will. If you make them apart from Him, you will never enjoy the fruit you are looking for.

Proverbs 27: Scripture

Do Not Boast about Tomorrow

1 Don't boast about tomorrow; for you don't know what a day may bring forth.

2 Let another man praise you, and not your own mouth; a stranger, and not your own lips.

3 A stone is heavy, and sand is a burden; but a fool's provocation is heavier than both.

4 Wrath is cruel, and anger is overwhelming; but who is able to stand before jealousy?

5 Better is open rebuke than hidden love.

6 Faithful are the wounds of a friend; although the kisses of an enemy are profuse.

7 A full soul loathes a honeycomb; but to a hungry soul, every bitter thing is sweet.

8 As a bird that wanders from her nest, so is a man who wanders from his home.

9 Perfume and incense bring joy to the heart; so does earnest counsel from a man's friend.

10 Don't forsake your friend and your father's friend. Don't go to your brother's house in the day of your disaster: better is a neighbor who is near than a distant brother.

11 Be wise, my son, and bring joy to my heart, then I can answer my tormentor.

12 A prudent man sees danger and takes refuge; but the simple pass on, and suffer for it.

13 Take his garment when he puts up collateral for a stranger. Hold it for a wayward woman!

14 He who blesses his neighbor with a loud voice early in the morning, it will be taken as a curse by him.

15 A continual dropping on a rainy day and a contentious wife are alike:

16 restraining her is like restraining the wind, or like grasping oil in his right hand.

17 Iron sharpens iron; so a man sharpens his friend's countenance.

18 Whoever tends the fig tree shall eat its fruit. He who looks after his master shall be honored.

19 As water reflects a face, so a man's heart reflects the man.

20 Sheol and Abaddon are never satisfied; and a man's eyes are never satisfied.

21 The crucible is for silver, and the furnace for gold; but man is refined by his praise.

22 Though you grind a fool in a mortar with a pestle along with grain, yet his foolishness will not be removed from him.

23 Know well the state of your flocks, and pay attention to your herds:

24 for riches are not forever, nor does even the crown endure to all generations.

25 The hay is removed, and the new growth appears, the grasses of the hills are gathered in.

26 The lambs are for your clothing, and the goats are the price of a field.

27 There will be plenty of goats' milk for your food, for your family's food, and for the nourishment of your servant girls.

Thoughts to Reflect Upon:

Why should we avoid boasting about ourselves? How does pride compromise our character? How can we surrender our plans to His perfect Will? Why is fellowship such an important discipline? How does it enrich our lives? Why is the company we keep so important?

Verse of the Day: 27/   Date:

_____
_____
_____

Journal/Notes Section-

_____
_____
_____
_____
_____
_____
_____
_____
_____
_____
_____
_____
_____
_____
_____
_____
_____
_____
_____
_____

Proverbs 28:
The Rulership of the Righteous

The wicked and the righteous are two opposing forces battling one another. The wicked have no regard for the law, but the righteous support justice. The wicked are cowards and "flee when no one pursues." They live in fear of being caught or having vengeance taken upon them. The righteous do not have to flee, as they have the covering of peace and Jesus watching over them.

The Book of Proverbs often contrasts the wicked with the righteous. This is done to teach us the stark differences between the ways of the world and the ways of God. This is emphasized so much throughout the Book of Proverbs that we come to embrace the way that we must live.

But why does God want to drill this into our heads? Because He loves us more than we could ever imagine, and He wants our eternal destiny to be spent with Him. He wants to see us come to salvation in Christ so we can be with Him forever.

A corrupt society will always praise the criminal. "Those who forsake the law praise the wicked; but those who keep the law contend with them." With the support of the Jews, the entire Roman court let the criminal Barabbas free in opposition to Jesus, a healer of people and light of the world.

Regardless of who our leaders are, we must pray for them. Even if we oppose the wicked, we must pray for them and love them into repentance. We don't oppose the wicked because we seek to destroy or hurt them. We oppose them for righteousness' sake and for the healing of our land.

Proverbs 28: Scripture

The Righteous Are as Bold as a Lion

1 The wicked flee when no one pursues; but the righteous are as bold as a lion.

2 In rebellion, a land has many rulers, but order is maintained by a man of understanding and knowledge.

3 A needy man who oppresses the poor is like a driving rain which leaves no crops.

4 Those who forsake the law praise the wicked; but those who keep the law contend with them.

5 Evil men don't understand justice; but those who seek Yahweh understand it fully.

6 Better is the poor who walks in his integrity, than he who is perverse in his ways, and he is rich.

7 Whoever keeps the law is a wise son; but he who is a companion of gluttons shames his father.

8 He who increases his wealth by excessive interest gathers it for one who has pity on the poor.

9 He who turns away his ear from hearing the law, even his prayer is an abomination.

10 Whoever causes the upright to go astray in an evil way, he will fall into his own trap; but the blameless will inherit good.

11 The rich man is wise in his own eyes; but the poor who has understanding sees through him.

12 When the righteous triumph, there is great glory; but when the wicked rise, men hide themselves.

13 He who conceals his sins doesn't prosper, but whoever confesses and renounces them finds mercy.

14 Blessed is the man who always fears; but one who hardens his heart falls into trouble.

15 As a roaring lion or a charging bear, so is a wicked ruler over helpless people.

16 A tyrannical ruler lacks judgment. One who hates ill-gotten gain will have long days.

17 A man who is tormented by life blood will be a fugitive until death; no one will support him.

18 Whoever walks blamelessly is kept safe; but one with perverse ways will fall suddenly.

19 One who works his land will have an abundance of food; but one who chases fantasies will have his fill of poverty.

20 A faithful man is rich with blessings; but one who is eager to be rich will not go unpunished.

21 To show partiality is not good; yet a man will do wrong for a piece of bread.

22 A stingy man hurries after riches, and doesn't know that poverty waits for him.

23 One who rebukes a man will afterward find more favor than one who flatters with the tongue.

24 Whoever robs his father or his mother, and says, "It's not wrong." He is a partner with a destroyer.

25 One who is greedy stirs up strife; but one who trusts in Yahweh will prosper.

26 One who trusts in himself is a fool; but one who walks in wisdom is kept safe.

27 One who gives to the poor has no lack; but one who closes his eyes will have many curses.

28 When the wicked rise, men hide themselves; but when they perish, the righteous thrive.

Thoughts to Reflect Upon:

How are the wicked and the righteous different? Why does the Book of Proverbs speak to these two opposing forces so often? How can we make sure we're among the righteous? Why should we always pray for our leaders, regardless of who they are?

Verse of the Day: 28/   Date:

_____
_____
_____

Journal/Notes Section-

Proverbs 29: Have Self-Control

When we receive criticism, we can either take it to the Lord in prayer following what the Word says, or we can be offended and walk away from the person who criticizes us. People may have ulterior motives, but we will know what to receive or discard if we are seeking the Lord.

God wants us to be righteous in our ways, not just for ourselves, but for the sake of society. "When the righteous thrive, the people rejoice; but when the wicked rule, the people groan." Wicked leaders are a curse to the people, always bringing destruction with their disregard for the truth. "The bloodthirsty hate a man of integrity; And they seek the life of the upright."

The righteous and the wicked are opposing forces, constantly at odds with one another. We are to be careful not to associate with those who give in to their selfish desires. We are called to minister, speak the truth, and bring that revelation to the lost, for, "Where there is no revelation, the people cast off restraint; but one who keeps the law is blessed." To mentor others and be a witness in Christ, we are to be wise in our emotions, never giving in to them on a whim. "A fool vents all of his anger, but a wise man brings himself under control."

This is where the differences between the ways of the world and the ways of God are clearly evident. According to God's design, we are to have control over our emotions. But the way of the world tells us that we should express ourselves at all costs, which only leads to a compromise of character. Just another illustration of why we must cling to the ways of God in this fallen world.

Proverbs 29: Scripture

The Stiff-Necked Will be Destroyed

1 He who is often rebuked and stiffens his neck will be destroyed suddenly, with no remedy.

2 When the righteous thrive, the people rejoice; but when the wicked rule, the people groan.

3 Whoever loves wisdom brings joy to his father; but a companion of prostitutes squanders his wealth.

4 The king by justice makes the land stable, but he who takes bribes tears it down.

5 A man who flatters his neighbor spreads a net for his feet.

6 An evil man is snared by his sin, but the righteous can sing and be glad.

7 The righteous care about justice for the poor. The wicked aren't concerned about knowledge.

8 Mockers stir up a city, but wise men turn away anger.

9 If a wise man goes to court with a foolish man, the fool rages or scoffs, and there is no peace.

10 The bloodthirsty hate a man of integrity; and they seek the life of the upright.

11 A fool vents all of his anger, but a wise man brings himself under control.

12 If a ruler listens to lies, all of his officials are wicked.

13 The poor man and the oppressor have this in common: Yahweh gives sight to the eyes of both.

14 The king who fairly judges the poor, his throne shall be established forever.

15 The rod of correction gives wisdom, but a child left to himself causes shame to his mother.

16 When the wicked increase, sin increases; but the righteous will see their downfall.

17 Correct your son, and he will give you peace; yes, he will bring delight to your soul.

18 Where there is no revelation, the people cast off restraint; but one who keeps the law is blessed.

19 A servant can't be corrected by words. Though he understands, yet he will not respond.

20 Do you see a man who is hasty in his words? There is more hope for a fool than for him.

21 He who pampers his servant from youth will have him become a son in the end.

22 An angry man stirs up strife, and a wrathful man abounds in sin.

23 A man's pride brings him low, but one of lowly spirit gains honor.

24 Whoever is an accomplice of a thief is an enemy of his own soul. He takes an oath, but dares not testify.

25 The fear of man proves to be a snare, but whoever puts his trust in Yahweh is kept safe.

26 Many seek the ruler's favor, but a man's justice comes from Yahweh.

27 A dishonest man detests the righteous, and the upright in their ways detest the wicked.

Thoughts to Reflect Upon:

How should we receive criticism? How can constructive criticism help us to grow in our faith? Why should we always be coachable? Why should we flee from the ways of the world? How are the ways of God different? How does prayerful obedience help us to follow Him?

Verse of the Day: 29/   Date:

_____
_____
_____

Journal/Notes Section-

_____
_____
_____
_____
_____
_____
_____
_____
_____
_____
_____
_____
_____
_____
_____
_____
_____

Proverbs 30: God's Word is Complete

Agur, the author credited with this chapter, starts with a confession of his own ignorance. He admits there is nothing he really knows. "Surely I am the most ignorant man and don't have a man's understanding. I have not learned wisdom, neither do I have the knowledge of the Holy One." This confession accentuates the value of the true wisdom which comes from God's Word.

God's Word is complete, and we are never to add to what God has already made whole. Many false teachers and man-made "religions" add to or subtract from God's Word. By doing so, they undermine God's word, which is already complete. "Every word of God is flawless. He is a shield to those who take refuge in him. Don't you add to his words, lest he reprove you, and you be found a liar." We should therefore obey the Lord with all our heart.

Agur adds that material things should never control us; rather, we should be content with having just what we need. "The leach has two daughters: Give and Give." There are many people who will take more and more from others without any thought beyond their selfish desires.

In many ways, our society has lifted up evil as good. The adulterous woman is considered independent, sexually free, and in control. "So is the way of an adulterous woman: She eats and wipes her mouth, And says, 'I have done nothing wrong.'" She may feel guiltless, but her ways lead to death.

We, as a people, have also elevated human wisdom and knowledge to an unhealthy, idolatrous level. We must take on the attitude of Agur, realizing that true knowledge and wisdom are the Lord's, not ours. No matter how much we learn or know, God's wisdom is above ours and is boundless.

Proverbs 30: Scripture

The Words of Agur: An Inspired Utterance

1 The words of Agur the son of Jakeh, the oracle: the man says to Ithiel, to Ithiel and Ucal:

2 "Surely I am the most ignorant man, and don't have a man's understanding.

3 I have not learned wisdom, neither do I have the knowledge of the Holy One.

4 Who has ascended up into heaven, and descended? Who has gathered the wind in his fists? Who has bound the waters in his garment? Who has established all the ends of the earth? What is his name, and what is his son's name, if you know?

5 "Every word of God is flawless. He is a shield to those who take refuge in him.

6 Don't you add to his words, lest he reprove you, and you be found a liar.

7 "Two things I have asked of you; don't deny me before I die:

8 Remove far from me falsehood and lies. Give me neither poverty nor riches. Feed me with the food that is needful for me;

9 lest I be full, deny you, and say, 'Who is Yahweh?' or lest I be poor, and steal, and so dishonor the name of my God.

10 "Don't slander a servant to his master, lest he curse you, and you be held guilty.

11 There is a generation that curses their father, and doesn't bless their mother.

12 There is a generation that is pure in their own eyes, yet are not washed from their filthiness.

13 There is a generation, oh how lofty are their eyes! Their eyelids are lifted up.

14 There is a generation whose teeth are like swords, and their jaws like knives, to devour the poor from the earth, and the needy from among men.

15 "The leach has two daughters: 'Give, give.' "There are three things that are never satisfied; four that don't say, 'Enough:'

16 Sheol, the barren womb; the earth that is not satisfied with water; and the fire that doesn't say, 'Enough.'

17 "The eye that mocks at his father, and scorns obedience to his mother: the ravens of the valley shall pick it out, the young eagles shall eat it.

18 "There are three things which are too amazing for me, four which I don't understand:

19 The way of an eagle in the air; the way of a serpent on a rock; the way of a ship in the midst of the sea; and the way of a man with a maiden.

20 "So is the way of an adulterous woman: she eats and wipes her mouth, and says, 'I have done nothing wrong.'

21 "For three things the earth tremble, and under four, it can't bear up:

22 For a servant when he is king; a fool when he is filled with food;

23 for an unloved woman when she is married; and a handmaid who is heir to her mistress.

24 "There are four things which are little on the earth, but they are exceedingly wise:

25 the ants are not a strong people, yet they provide their food in the summer.

26 The conies are but a feeble folk, yet make they their houses in the rocks.

27 The locusts have no king, yet they advance in ranks.

28 You can catch a lizard with your hands, yet it is in kings' palaces.

29 "There are three things which are stately in their march, four which are stately in going:

30 The lion, which is mightiest among animals, and doesn't turn away for any;

31 the greyhound, the male goat also; and the king against whom there is no rising up.

32 "If you have done foolishly in lifting up yourself, or if you have thought evil, put your hand over your mouth.

33 For as the churning of milk brings forth butter, and the wringing of the nose brings forth blood; so the forcing of wrath brings forth strife."

Thoughts to Reflect Upon:

How is the Word of God complete? Why should we never add to or take away from it? Why should we never let material things control us? How has the world lifted up what is evil and shunned what is good? Why is elevating human wisdom highly dangerous?

Verse of the Day: 30/   Date:

Journal/Notes Section-

Proverbs 31: The God-Fearing Woman

Perhaps the most famous chapter in Proverbs is from King Lemuel, who gained wisdom from his mother. She instilled in him sound advice on how to avoid destruction through promiscuity and excessive alcohol, lest through drinking he should forget the law and pervert justice.

Many in this world do not follow this advice. They live lives of excess. While it may sound attractive from the outside, looking in, it's not the way we want to live. Ultimately, it leads to our ruin. Once we've tumbled down that rabbit hole, we realize that it's not as wonderful as it seems to be. All we will be left with is our broken and hollow selves.

The second part of the chapter is the famous "Proverbs 31 woman." Any man fortunate enough to find such a woman is truly blessed. She cares for the needs of her entire household, including the servants. She even has her own private ventures to add to the family fund. Her husband trusts implicitly in her judgment, and, through her support, he rises to become a respected leader in the city.

Her wisdom, strength, and dignity enable her family to feel secure and protected even at the prospect of hard times: "She is not afraid of the snow for her household; For all her household are clothed with scarlet." I believe the scarlet covering is prophetic, speaking of the blood of Jesus, for she is a God-fearing woman. "Charm is deceitful, and beauty is vain; But a woman who fears Yahweh, she shall be praised."

This verse paints a picture of what it means to be a godly woman. This is what every Christian woman should strive to be, and what every Christian man should seek in a partner.

Proverbs 31: Scripture

The Words of King Lemuel

1 The words of king Lemuel; the oracle which his mother taught him.

2 "Oh, my son!" Oh, son of my womb! Oh, son of my vows!

3 Don't give your strength to women, nor your ways to that which destroys kings.

4 It is not for kings, Lemuel; it is not for kings to drink wine; Nor for princes to say, 'Where is strong drink?'

5 Lest they drink, and forget the law, and pervert the justice due to anyone who is afflicted.

6 Give strong drink to him who is ready to perish; And wine to the bitter in soul:

7 Let him drink, and forget his poverty, and remember his misery no more.

8 Open your mouth for the mute, In the cause of all who are left desolate.

9 Open your mouth, judge righteously, and serve justice to the poor and needy."

The Virtues of a Noble Woman

10 Who can find a worthy woman? For her price is far above rubies.

11 The heart of her husband trusts in her. He shall have no lack of gain.

12 She does him good, and not harm, All the days of her life.

13 She seeks wool and flax and works eagerly with her hands.

14 She is like the merchant ships. She brings her bread from afar.

15 She rises also while it is yet night, Gives food to her household, And their task to her servant girls.

16 She considers a field, and buys it. With the fruit of her hands, she plants a vineyard.

17 She girds her loins with strength, and makes her arms strong.

18 She perceives that her merchandise is profitable. Her lamp doesn't go out by night.

19 She lays her hands to the distaff, and her hands hold the spindle.

20 She stretches out her hand to the poor; Yes, she reaches forth her hands to the needy.

21 She is not afraid of the snow for her household; For all her household are clothed with scarlet.

22 She makes for herself carpets of tapestry. Her clothing is fine linen and purple.

23 Her husband is respected in the gates, when he sits among the elders of the land.

24 She makes linen garments and sells them and delivers sashes to the merchant.

25 Strength and dignity are her clothing. She laughs at the time to come.

26 She opens her mouth with wisdom. Instruction of faithfulness is on her tongue.

27 She looks well to the ways of her household, and doesn't eat the bread of idleness.

28 Her children rise up and call her blessed. Her husband also praises her:

29 "Many women do noble things, but you excel them all."

30 Charm is deceitful, and beauty is vain; But a woman who fears Yahweh, she shall be praised.

31 Give her of the fruit of her hands; Let her works praise her in the gates.

Thoughts to Reflect Upon:

Why is it important that we follow godly advice? Why do so many struggle with that? Why is the Proverbs 31 woman as described in this chapter such a virtuous example to look to? How can you best emulate her godly character in your life?

Verse of the Day: 31/   Date:

_____
_____
_____

Journal/Notes Section-

_____
_____
_____
_____
_____
_____
_____
_____
_____
_____
_____
_____
_____
_____
_____
_____
_____
_____
_____
_____

SUMMARY:

What an amazing collection of wise sayings and teachings! God has given us practical advice on relationships, work, money, and moral conduct. It is clear God simply knows best, so let us strive to obtain wisdom, gain understanding, and live righteously.

After reading Proverbs, I feel all the "wiser." For me, I did not learn as much as I needed the "rod" of correction. The Word of God has made me sharper than ever before. I cannot help but think you are also wiser. My prayer is for you to obtain more and more godly wisdom in your journey to becoming more Christ-like.

Thank you for reading my commentaries. If you're interested in reflecting deeper on wisdom and further discussion, feel free to join our Facebook group by emailing:

gs@christophercoopersmith.com.

Sincerely,

Christopher S. Coopersmith

WANT MORE?

Building a relationship with my readers is the absolute best thing about writing. I occasionally send newsletters detailing new releases, special offers, and other news related to my *Guiding Scripture* series.

And if you sign up for the mailing list, I'll send you all this free material:

1. "A Guide to The Three Letters of John & Jude" – free eBook
2. "Daily Proverbs Checklist" – a checklist for the book of Proverbs
3. "5 Questions to Fully Understand a Bible Verse" – understanding what you are reading is vital; these questions will help.
4. "Leaders Daily Checklist" – God calls us to be leaders. We need to improve our leadership to set an example.

You can get the free eBook, Proverbs checklist, questions, and leadership checklist by signing up at https://christophercoopersmith.com/guiding-scripture-series/

Did you learn something new?
Help other like-minded readers find this book.

Reviews are the most powerful tools in my arsenal for getting my books connected to other like-minded readers. I do not have the same financial resources as a larger publishing house.

However, I do have something much more valuable: **a dedicated group of readers who support my work.**

Honest reviews from my readers help my books gain the attention of new audiences.

If you've enjoyed this book, would you kindly consider leaving a review on the relevant page? Even a short review can make a big difference in helping me reach more readers.

Thank you for your support!

Click here to leave a short one-minute review.

Or Scan This QR

Author

I'm a sinner redeemed by Christ's grace. God has fueled a passionate fire in me to build a Christ-centered community. I have had the privilege of serving the community both locally and abroad. To date, I have spread the good news in over 11 different countries. My one true purpose is to use my God-given gifts to lead others to redemption.

You can send an email to gs@christophercoopersmith.com to join our private Facebook group to establish a Christian community around God's wisdom. I hope you enjoy this journal.

For those of you who are brave enough, tell me what you think about this book.

Email: gs@christophercoopersmith.com.

I am for real. I am an actual human being.

OTHER TITLES BY CHRISTOPHER COOPERSMITH

Have you read them all?

The Three Letters of John & Jude

This Journey through *The Letters of John and Jude* provides a roadmap to developing a deeper understanding of scripture and all God's teachings. Like a salve for the soul, it is filled with much-needed wisdom, lessons, and stories that will resonate with you and what's happening in your life.

Read Now: Scan this QR

Ruth & Esther: Courageous Faith

Courageous Faith is a meticulous examination of what these two legendary women had in common. Adding more insights from other Old Testament scriptures, Coopersmith shines a light on the critical roles Ruth and Esther played in the Messiah's family tree and in preserving the Jewish nation. And as you read along, you'll fall upon a wealth of hope and joy that supports your path to becoming a powerful disciple of Christ.

Read Now: Scan this QR

Hebrews: Christ Never Leaves Us

Christ Never Leaves Us is a meticulous examination of the themes, reassurances, and admonitions contained in this missive to new Messianic converts. Using journal questions and comprehensive scripture references, Coopersmith reveals how to lean on messages to ancient Christians for hope in your modern-day walk with Jehovah. And by pouring through this study with an open heart, you'll soon be hearing God's voice with crystal clarity.

Read Now: Scan this QR

ACKNOWLEDGMENTS

I dedicate this book to Phil and Ruth Rouchard, two humble servants of the Lord who have had significant impact on the lives of believers. Thank you for selflessly pouring into the lives of many. Everyone you meet is eternally grateful.

Copyright 2022

Editor: Zachary Wessell

Copy Editor: Fleur Vaz & Vickie Spencer

Proofreaders: Kerrie McLoughlin & Changfang Wang

Cover Design: pro-ebookcovers & Damonza

eBook: ISBN – 978-1-955922-15-9

Paperback: ISBN – 978-1-955922-16-6

Hardcover: ISBN – 978-1-955922-17-3

The author has made every possible effort to ensure the accuracy of the information presented in this book. However, the information herein is sold without warranty, either expressed or implied. The author, publisher, dealer, or distributor of this book will not be held liable for any damages caused directly or indirectly by the instructions or information contained in this book. You are encouraged to seek professional advice before taking any action mentioned herein.

In accordance with the U.S. Copyright Act of 1976, the scanning, uploading, and electronic sharing of any part of this book without the publisher's permission is unlawful piracy and theft of the author's intellectual property. If you would like to use material from this book (other than for review purposes), you can obtain prior written permission by contacting the author. Thank you for your support of the author's rights.

Notice of Rights: All rights reserved. No part of this book may be reproduced or transmitted in any form, electronic, mechanical, photocopy, recording, or other, without the author's prior and express written permission except for brief cited quotes. Thank you for respecting property rights.

Permission: For information on getting permission for reprints and excerpts, contact:

ccoopersmith@christophercoopersmith.com

Bibliography

Got Questions. "Who Was King Lemuel in Proverbs 31?" Accessed April 11, 2021. https://www.gotquestions.org/King-Lemuel.html

Hamer Smith, Sandra. "Who Wrote Proverbs?" *Bible Study Tools*, March 17, 2021. https://www.biblestudytools.com/bible-study/topical-studies/who-wrote-proverbs.html

Heiser, Michael S. "Who Wrote the Book of Proverbs?" *Bible Study Magazine*, November 16, 2017. https://www.biblestudymagazine.com/bible-study-magazine-blog/2017/11/16/who-wrote-the-book-of-proverbs

Insight for Living. "Proverbs." Accessed April 11, 2021. https://www.insight.org/resources/bible/the-wisdom-books/proverbs

Jewish Virtual Library. "King Solomon." Accessed April 11, 2021. https://www.jewishvirtuallibrary.org/king-solomon

Mark, Joshua J. "Yahweh." *World History Encyclopedia*, October 22, 2018. https://www.ancient.eu/Yahweh/

Rust, Brittany. "9 Interesting Things You Might Not Know About King Solomon." Crosswalk.com, November 26, 2019. https://www.crosswalk.com/about-crosswalk.html

StudyLight.org. "Proverbs 2." Accessed April 11, 2021.
    https://www.studylight.org/commentaries/eng/pet/proverbs-2.html

The Editors of Encyclopedia Britannica. "Yahweh." *Encyclopedia Britannica*. Accessed April 11, 2021.
    https://www.britannica.com/topic/Yahweh

Total History. "Proverbs Chapter 1." Accessed April 11, 2021.
    https://totallyhistory.com/proverbs-chapter-1/

*Bibliography sources cited by J.A. Rapps

Made in the USA
Las Vegas, NV
04 May 2025